BHARATIYA SAKSHYA ADHINIYAM 2023

BARE ACT   2024

BHARATIYA SAKSHYA ADHINIYAM 2023

with

A Comparative Study of Bharatiya Sakshya Adhiniyam 2023 & Indian Evidence Act 1872

RUPA

Published by
Rupa Publications India Pvt. Ltd 2024
7/16, Ansari Road, Daryaganj
New Delhi 110002

Sales centres:
Bengaluru Chennai
Hyderabad Jaipur Kathmandu
Kolkata Mumbai Prayagraj

P-ISBN: 978-93-6156-988-3
E-ISBN: 978-93-6156-141-2

First impression 2024

10 9 8 7 6 5 4 3 2 1

Printed in India

CONTENTS

Admissions

Statements by persons who cannot be called as witnesses

Statements made under special circumstances

How much of a statement is to be proved

Judgments of Courts when relevant

Opinions of third persons when relevant

Character when relevant

PART III

ON PROOF

Chapter III
FACTS WHICH NEED NOT BE PROVED

Chapter IV
OF ORAL EVIDENCE

Chapter V
OF DOCUMENTARY EVIDENCE

Public documents

Chapter VI
OF THE EXCLUSION OF ORAL EVIDENCE BY DOCUMENTARY EVIDENCE

PART IV
PRODUCTION AND EFFECT OF EVIDENCE

Chapter VII
OF THE BURDEN OF PROOF

Chapter VIII
ESTOPPEL

Chapter IX
OF WITNESSES

Chapter X
OF EXAMINATION OF WITNESSES

Chapter XI
OF IMPROPER ADMISSION AND
REJECTION OF EVIDENCE

Chapter XII
REPEAL AND SAVINGS

THE BHARATIYA SAKSHYA ADHINIYAM, 2023
NO. 47 OF 2023

[*25th December,* 2023.]

An Act to consolidate and to provide for general
rules and principles of evidence for fair trial.

BE it enacted by Parliament in the Seventy-fourth Year of the Republic of India as follows:—

PART I

Chapter I

PRELIMINARY

Short title, application and commencement.

1. (1) This Act may be called the Bharatiya Sakshya Adhiniyam, 2023.

(2) It applies to all judicial proceedings in or before any Court, including Courts-martial, but not to affidavits presented to any Court or officer, nor to proceedings before an arbitrator.

(3) It shall come into force on such date as the Central Government may, by notification in the Official Gazette, appoint.

Definitions.

2. (1) In this Adhiniyam, unless the context otherwise requires,—

    (*a*) "Court" includes all Judges and Magistrates, and all persons, except arbitrators, legally authorised to take evidence;

    (*b*) "conclusive proof" means when one fact is declared by this Adhiniyam to be conclusive proof of another, the Court shall, on proof of the one fact, regard the other as proved, and shall not allow evidence to be given for the purpose of disproving it;

    (*c*) "disproved" in relation to a fact, means when, after considering the matters before it, the Court either believes that it does not exist, or considers its non-existence so probable that a prudent man ought, under the circumstances of the particular case, to act upon the supposition that it does not exist;

(*d*) "document" means any matter expressed or described or otherwise recorded upon any substance by means of letters, figures or marks or any other means or by more than one of those means, intended to be used, or which may be used, for the purpose of recording that matter and includes electronic and digital records.

Illustrations.

(i)   A writing is a document.

(ii)   Words printed, lithographed or photographed are documents.

(iii) A map or plan is a document.

(iv) An inscription on a metal plate or stone is a document.

(v)   A caricature is a document.

(vi) An electronic record on emails, server logs, documents on computers, laptop or smartphone, messages, websites, locational evidence and voice mail messages stored on digital devices are documents;

(*e*) "evidence" means and includes—

(i)   all statements including statements given electronically which the Court permits or requires to be made before it by witnesses in relation to matters of fact under inquiry and such statements are called oral evidence;

(ii) all documents including electronic or digital records produced for the inspection of the Court and such documents are called documentary evidence;

(*f*) "fact" means and includes—

(i)   any thing, state of things, or relation of things, capable of being perceived by the senses;

(ii) any mental condition of which any person is conscious.

Illustrations.

(i)   That there are certain objects arranged in a certain order in a certain place, is a fact.

(ii)   That a person heard or saw something, is a fact.

(iii) That a person said certain words, is a fact.

(iv) That a person holds a certain opinion, has a certain intention, acts in good faith, or fraudulently, or uses a particular word in a particular sense, or is or was at a specified time conscious of a particular sensation, is a fact;

(*g*) "facts in issue" means and includes any fact from which, either by itself or in connection with other facts, the existence, non-existence, nature or extent of any right, liability or disability, asserted or denied in any suit or proceeding, necessarily follows.

Explanation.—Whenever, under the provisions of the law for the time being in force relating to civil procedure, any Court records an issue of fact, the fact to be asserted or denied in the answer to such issue is a fact in issue.

Illustrations.

A is accused of the murder of B. At his trial, the following facts may be in issue:—

    (i)   That A caused B's death.

    (ii)   That A intended to cause B's death.

    (iii)   That A had received grave and sudden provocation from B.

    (iv)   That A, at the time of doing the act which caused B's death, was, by reason of unsoundness of mind, incapable of knowing its nature;

(*h*) "may presume".—Whenever it is provided by this Adhiniyam that the Court may presume a fact, it may either regard such fact as proved, unless and until it is disproved or may call for proof of it;

(*i*) "not proved".—A fact is said to be not proved when it is neither proved nor disproved;

(*j*) "proved".—A fact is said to be proved when, after considering the matters before it, the Court either believes it to exist, or considers its existence so probable that a prudent man ought, under the circumstances of the particular case, to act upon the supposition that it exists;

(*k*) "relevant".—A fact is said to be relevant to another when it is connected with the other in any of the ways referred to in the provisions of this Adhiniyam relating to the relevancy of facts;

(*l*) "shall presume".—Whenever it is directed by this Adhiniyam that the Court shall presume a fact, it shall regard such fact as proved, unless and until it is disproved.

(2) Words and expressions used herein and not defined but defined in the Information Technology Act, 2000, (21 of 2000) the Bharatiya Nagarik Suraksha Sanhita, 2023 and the Bharatiya Nyaya Sanhita, 2023 shall have the same meanings as assigned to them in the said Act and Sanhitas.

PART II

Chapter II

RELEVANCY OF FACTS

Evidence may be given of facts in issue and relevant facts.

3. Evidence may be given in any suit or proceeding of the existence or non-existence of every fact in issue and of such other facts as are hereinafter declared to be relevant, and of no others.

Explanation.—This section shall not enable any person to give evidence of a fact which he is disentitled to prove by any provision of the law for the time being in force relating to civil procedure.

Illustrations.

(*a*) A is tried for the murder of B by beating him with a club with the intention of causing his death.
  At A's trial the following facts are in issue:—
    A's beating B with the club;
    A's causing B's death by such beating;
    A's intention to cause B's death.

(*b*) A suitor does not bring with him, and have in readiness for production at the first hearing of the case, a bond on which he relies. This section does not enable him to produce the bond or prove its contents at a subsequent stage of the proceedings, otherwise than in accordance with the conditions prescribed by the Code of Civil Procedure, 1908 (5 of 1908).

Closely connected facts

Relevancy of facts forming part of same transaction.

4. Facts which, though not in issue, are so connected with a fact in issue or a relevant fact as to form part of the same transaction, are relevant, whether they occurred at the same time and place or at different times and places.

Illustrations.

(*a*) A is accused of the murder of B by beating him. Whatever was said or done by A or B or the bystanders at the beating, or so shortly before or after it as to form part of the transaction, is a relevant fact.

(*b*) A is accused of waging war against the Government of India by taking part in an armed insurrection in which property is destroyed, troops are attacked and jails are broken open. The occurrence of these facts is relevant, as forming part of the general transaction, though A may not have been present at all of them.

(*c*) A sues B for a libel contained in a letter forming part of a correspondence. Letters between the parties relating to the subject out of which the libel arose, and forming part of the correspondence in which it is contained, are relevant facts, though they do not contain the libel itself.

(*d*) The question is, whether certain goods ordered from B were delivered to A. The goods were delivered to several intermediate persons successively. Each delivery is a relevant fact.

Facts which are occasion, cause or effect of facts in issue or relevant facts.

5. Facts which are the occasion, cause or effect, immediate or otherwise, of relevant facts, or facts in issue, or which constitute the state of things under which they happened, or which afforded an opportunity for their occurrence or transaction, are relevant.

Illustrations.

(*a*) The question is, whether A robbed B. The facts that, shortly before the robbery, B went to a fair with money in his possession, and that he showed it, or mentioned the fact that he had it, to third persons, are relevant.

(*b*) The question is, whether A murdered B. Marks on the ground, produced by a struggle at or near the place where the murder was committed, are relevant facts.

(*c*) The question is, whether A poisoned B. The state of B's health before the symptoms ascribed to poison, and habits of B, known to A, which afforded an opportunity for the administration of poison, are relevant facts.

Motive, preparation and previous or subsequent conduct.

6. (1) Any fact is relevant which shows or constitutes a motive or preparation for any fact in issue or relevant fact.

(2) The conduct of any party, or of any agent to any party, to any suit or proceeding, in reference to such suit or proceeding, or in reference to any fact in issue therein or relevant thereto, and the conduct of any person, an offence against whom is the subject of any proceeding, is relevant, if such conduct influences or is influenced by any fact in issue or relevant fact, and whether it was previous or subsequent thereto.

Explanation 1.—The word "conduct" in this section does not include statements, unless those statements accompany and explain acts other than statements; but this explanation is not to affect the relevancy of statements under any other section of this Adhiniyam.

Explanation 2.—When the conduct of any person is relevant, any statement made to him or in his presence and hearing, which affects such conduct, is relevant.

Illustrations.

(*a*) A is tried for the murder of B. The facts that A murdered C, that B knew that A had murdered C, and that B had tried to extort money from A by threatening to make his knowledge public, are relevant.

(*b*) A sues B upon a bond for the payment of money. B denies the making of the bond. The fact that, at the time when the bond was alleged to be made, B required money for a particular purpose, is relevant.

(*c*) A is tried for the murder of B by poison. The fact that, before the death of B, A procured poison similar to that which was administered to B, is relevant.

(*d*) The question is, whether a certain document is the will of A. The facts that, not long before, the date of the alleged will, A made inquiry into matters to which the provisions of the alleged will relate; that he consulted advocates in reference to making the will, and that he caused drafts of other wills to be prepared, of which he did not approve, are relevant.

(*e*) A is accused of a crime. The facts that, either before, or at the time of, or after the alleged crime, A provided evidence which would tend to give to the facts of the case an appearance favourable to himself, or that he destroyed or concealed evidence, or prevented the presence or procured the absence of persons who might have been witnesses, or suborned persons to give false evidence respecting it, are relevant.

(*f*) The question is, whether A robbed B. The facts that, after B was robbed, C said in A's presence—"the police are coming to look for the person who robbed B", and that immediately afterwards A ran away, are relevant.

(*g*) The question is, whether A owes B ten thousand rupees. The facts that A asked C to lend him money, and that D said to C in A's presence and hearing—"I advise you not to trust A, for he owes B ten thousand rupees", and that A went away without making any answer, are relevant facts.

(*h*) The question is, whether A committed a crime. The fact that A absconded, after receiving a letter, warning A that inquiry was being made for the criminal, and the contents of the letter, are relevant.

(*i*) A is accused of a crime. The facts that, after the commission of the alleged crime, A absconded, or was in possession of property or the proceeds of property acquired by the crime, or attempted to conceal things which were or might have been used in committing it, are relevant.

(*j*) The question is, whether A was raped. The fact that, shortly after the alleged rape, A made a complaint relating to the crime, the circumstances under which, and the terms in which, the complaint was made, are relevant. The fact that, without making a complaint, A said that A had been raped is not relevant as conduct under this section, though it may be relevant as a dying declaration under clause (*a*) of section 26, or as corroborative evidence under section 160.

(*k*) The question is, whether A was robbed. The fact that, soon after the alleged robbery, A made a complaint relating to the offence, the circumstances under which, and the terms in which, the complaint was made, are relevant. The fact that A said he had been robbed, without making any complaint, is not relevant, as conduct under this section, though it may be relevant as a dying declaration under clause (*a*) of section 26, or as corroborative evidence under section 160.

Facts necessary to explain or introduce fact in issue or relevant facts.

7. Facts necessary to explain or introduce a fact in issue or relevant fact, or which support or rebut an inference suggested by a fact in issue or a relevant fact, or which establish the identity of anything, or person whose identity, is relevant, or fix the time or place at which any fact in issue or relevant fact happened, or which show the relation of parties by whom any such fact was transacted, are relevant in so far as they are necessary for that purpose.

Illustrations.

(*a*) The question is, whether a given document is the will of A. The state of A's property and of his family at the date of the alleged will may be relevant facts.

(*b*) A sues B for a libel imputing disgraceful conduct to A; B affirms that the matter alleged to be libellous is true. The position and relations of the parties at the time when the libel was published may be relevant facts as introductory to the facts in issue. The particulars of a dispute between A and B about a matter unconnected with the alleged libel are irrelevant, though the fact that there was a dispute may be relevant if it affected the relations between A and B.

(*c*) A is accused of a crime. The fact that, soon after the commission of the crime, A absconded from his house, is relevant under section 6, as conduct subsequent to and affected by facts in issue. The fact that, at the time when he left home, A had sudden and urgent business at the place to which he went, is relevant, as tending to explain the fact that he left home suddenly. The details of the business on which he left are not relevant, except in so far as they are necessary to show that the business was sudden and urgent.

(*d*) A sues B for inducing C to break a contract of service made by him with A. C, on leaving A's service, says to A—"I am leaving you because B has made me a better offer". This statement is a relevant fact as explanatory of C's conduct, which is relevant as a fact in issue.

(*e*) A, accused of theft, is seen to give the stolen property to B, who is seen to give it to A's wife. B says as he delivers it—"A says you are to hide this". B's statement is relevant as explanatory of a fact which is part of the transaction.

(*f*) A is tried for a riot and is proved to have marched at the head of a mob. The cries of the mob are relevant as explanatory of the nature of the transaction.

Things said or done by conspirator in reference to common design.

8. Where there is reasonable ground to believe that two or more persons have conspired together to commit an offence or an actionable wrong, anything said, done or written by any one of such persons in reference to their common intention, after the time when such intention was first entertained by any one of them, is a relevant fact as against each of the persons believed to be so conspiring, as well for the purpose of proving the existence of the conspiracy as for the purpose of showing that any such person was a party to it.

Illustration.

Reasonable ground exists for believing that A has joined in a conspiracy to wage war against the State.

The facts that B procured arms in Europe for the purpose of the conspiracy, C collected money in Kolkata for a like object, D persuaded persons to join the conspiracy in Mumbai, E published writings advocating the object in view at Agra, and F transmitted from Delhi to G at Singapore the money which C had collected at Kolkata, and the contents of a letter written by H giving an account of the conspiracy, are each relevant, both to prove the existence of the conspiracy, and to prove A's complicity in it, although he may have been ignorant of all of them, and although the persons by whom they were done were strangers to him, and although they may have taken place before he joined the conspiracy or after he left it.

When facts not otherwise relevant become relevant.

9. Facts not otherwise relevant are relevant—
    (1) if they are inconsistent with any fact in issue or relevant fact;
    (2) if by themselves or in connection with other facts they make the existence or non-existence of any fact in issue or relevant fact highly probable or improbable.

Illustrations.

    (*a*) The question is, whether A committed a crime at Chennai on a certain day. The fact that, on that day, A was at Ladakh is relevant. The fact that, near the time when the crime was committed, A was at a distance from the place where it was committed, which would render it highly improbable, though not impossible, that he committed it, is relevant.

    (*b*) The question is, whether A committed a crime. The circumstances are such that the crime must have been committed either by A, B, C or D. Every fact which shows that the crime could have been committed by no one else, and that it was not committed by either B, C or D, is relevant.

Facts tending to enable Court to determine amount are relevant in suits for damages.

10. In suits in which damages are claimed, any fact which will enable the Court to determine the amount of damages which ought to be awarded, is relevant.

Facts relevant when right or custom is in question.

11. Where the question is as to the existence of any right or custom, the following facts are relevant—
    (*a*) any transaction by which the right or custom in question was created, claimed, modified, recognised, asserted or denied, or which was inconsistent with its existence;
    (*b*) particular instances in which the right or custom was claimed,

recognised or exercised, or in which its exercise was disputed, asserted or departed from.

Illustration.

The question is, whether A has a right to a fishery. A deed conferring the fishery on A's ancestors, a mortgage of the fishery by A's father, a subsequent grant of the fishery by A's father, irreconcilable with the mortgage, particular instances in which A's father exercised the right, or in which the exercise of the right was stopped by A's neighbours, are relevant facts.

Facts showing existence of state of mind, or of body or bodily feeling.

12. Facts showing the existence of any state of mind, such as intention, knowledge, good faith, negligence, rashness, ill-will or goodwill towards any particular person, or showing the existence of any state of body or bodily feeling, are relevant, when the existence of any such state of mind or body or bodily feeling is in issue or relevant.

Explanation 1.—A fact relevant as showing the existence of a relevant state of mind must show that the state of mind exists, not generally, but in reference to the particular matter in question.

Explanation 2.—But where, upon the trial of a person accused of an offence, the previous commission by the accused of an offence is relevant within the meaning of this section, the previous conviction of such person shall also be a relevant fact.

Illustrations.

(*a*) A is accused of receiving stolen goods knowing them to be stolen. It is proved that he was in possession of a particular stolen article. The fact that, at the same time, he was in possession of many other stolen articles is relevant, as tending to show that he knew each and all of the articles of which he was in possession to be stolen.

(*b*) A is accused of fraudulently delivering to another person a counterfeit currency which, at the time when he delivered it, he knew to be counterfeit. The fact that, at the time of its delivery, A was possessed of a number of other pieces of counterfeit currency is relevant. The fact that A had been previously convicted of delivering to another person as genuine a counterfeit currency knowing it to be counterfeit is relevant.

(*c*) A sues B for damage done by a dog of B's, which B knew to be ferocious. The fact that the dog had previously bitten X, Y and Z, and that they had made complaints to B, are relevant.

(*d*) The question is, whether A, the acceptor of a bill of exchange, knew that the name of the payee was fictitious. The fact that A had accepted other bills drawn in the same manner before they could have been transmitted to him by the payee if the payee had been a real person, is relevant, as showing that A knew that the payee was a fictitious person.

(*e*) A is accused of defaming B by publishing an imputation intended to harm the reputation of B. The fact of previous publications by A respecting B, showing ill-will on the part of A towards B is relevant, as proving A's intention to harm B's reputation by the particular publication in question. The facts that there was no previous quarrel between A and B, and that A repeated the matter complained of as he heard it, are relevant, as showing that A did not intend to harm the reputation of B.

(*f*) A is sued by B for fraudulently representing to B that C was solvent, whereby B, being induced to trust C, who was insolvent, suffered loss. The fact that, at the time when A represented C to be solvent, C was supposed to be solvent by his neighbours and by persons dealing with him, is relevant, as showing that A made the representation in good faith.

(*g*) A is sued by B for the price of work done by B, upon a house of which A is owner, by the order of C, a contractor. A's defence is that B's contract was with C. The fact that A paid C for the work in question is relevant, as proving that A did, in good faith, make over to C the management of the work in question, so that C was in a position to contract with B on C's own account, and not as agent for A.

(*h*) A is accused of the dishonest misappropriation of property which he had found, and the question is whether, when he appropriated it, he believed in good faith that the real owner could not be found. The fact that public notice of the loss of the property had been given in the place where A was, is relevant, as showing that A did not in good faith believe that the real owner of the property could not be found. The fact that A knew, or had reason to believe, that the notice was given fraudulently by C, who had heard of the loss of the property and wished to set up a false claim to it, is relevant, as showing that the fact that A knew of the notice did not disprove A's good faith.

(*i*) A is charged with shooting at B with intent to kill him. In order to show A's intent, the fact of A's having previously shot at B may be proved.

(*j*) A is charged with sending threatening letters to B. Threatening letters previously sent by A to B may be proved, as showing the intention of the letters.

(*k*) The question is, whether A has been guilty of cruelty towards B, his wife. Expressions of their feeling towards each other shortly before or after the alleged cruelty are relevant facts.

(*l*) The question is, whether A's death was caused by poison. Statements made by A during his illness as to his symptoms are relevant facts.

(*m*) The question is, what was the state of A's health at the time when an assurance on his life was effected. Statements made by A as to the state of his health at or near the time in question are relevant facts.

(*n*) A sues B for negligence in providing him with a car for hire not reasonably fit for use, whereby A was injured. The fact that B's attention was drawn on other occasions to the defect of that particular car is relevant. The fact that B was habitually negligent about the cars which he let to hire is irrelevant.

(*o*) A is tried for the murder of B by intentionally shooting him dead. The fact that A on other occasions shot at B is relevant as showing his intention to shoot B. The fact that A was in the habit of shooting at people with intent to murder them is irrelevant.

(*p*) A is tried for a crime. The fact that he said something indicating an intention to commit that particular crime is relevant. The fact that he said something indicating a general disposition to commit crimes of that class is irrelevant.

Facts bearing on question whether act was accidental or intentional.

13. When there is a question whether an act was accidental or intentional, or done with a particular knowledge or intention, the fact that such act formed part of a series of similar occurrences, in each of which the person doing the act was concerned, is relevant.

Illustrations.

(*a*) A is accused of burning down his house in order to obtain money for which it is insured. The facts that A lived in several houses successively each of which he insured, in each of which a fire occurred, and after each of which fires A received payment from a different insurance company, are relevant, as tending to show that the fires were not accidental.

(*b*) A is employed to receive money from the debtors of B. It is A's duty to make entries in a book showing the amounts received by him. He makes an entry showing that on a particular occasion he received less than he really did receive. The question is, whether this false entry was accidental or intentional. The facts that other entries made by A in the same book are false, and that the false entry is in each case in favour of A, are relevant.

(*c*) A is accused of fraudulently delivering to B a counterfeit currency. The question is, whether the delivery of the currency was accidental. The facts that, soon before or soon after the delivery to B, A delivered counterfeit currency to C, D and E are relevant, as showing that the delivery to B was not accidental.

Existence of course of business when relevant.

14. When there is a question whether a particular act was done, the existence of any course of business, according to which it naturally would have been done, is a relevant fact.

Illustrations.

(*a*) The question is, whether a particular letter was dispatched. The facts that it was the ordinary course of business for all letters put in a certain place to be carried to the post, and that particular letter was put in that place are relevant.

(*b*) The question is, whether a particular letter reached A. The facts that it was posted in due course, and was not returned through the Return Letter Office, are relevant.

Admissions

Admission defined.

15. An admission is a statement, oral or documentary or contained in electronic form, which suggests any inference as to any fact in issue or relevant fact, and which is made by any of the persons, and under the circumstances, hereinafter mentioned.

Admission by party to proceeding or his agent.

16. (1) Statements made by a party to the proceeding, or by an agent to any such party, whom the Court regards, under the circumstances of the case, as expressly or impliedly authorised by him to make them, are admissions.

(2) Statements made by—

(i) parties to suits suing or sued in a representative character, are not admissions, unless they were made while the party making them held that character; or

(ii) (*a*) persons who have any proprietary or pecuniary interest in the subject matter of the proceeding, and who make the statement in their character of persons so interested; or

(*b*) persons from whom the parties to the suit have derived their interest in the subject matter of the suit,

are admissions, if they are made during the continuance of the interest of the persons making the statements.

Admissions by persons whose position must be proved as against party to suit.

17. Statements made by persons whose position or liability, it is necessary to prove as against any party to the suit, are admissions, if such statements would be relevant as against such persons in relation to such position or liability in a suit brought by or against them, and if they are made whilst the person making them occupies such position or is subject to such liability.

Illustration.

A undertakes to collect rents for B. B sues A for not collecting rent due from C to B. A denies that rent was due from C to B. A statement by C that he owed B rent is an admission, and is a relevant fact as against A, if A denies that C did owe rent to B.

Admissions by persons expressly referred to by party to suit.

18. Statements made by persons to whom a party to the suit has expressly referred for information in reference to a matter in dispute are admissions.

Illustration.

The question is, whether a horse sold by A to B is sound.

A says to B—"Go and ask C, C knows all about it". C's statement is an admission.

Proof of admissions against persons making them, and by or on their behalf.

19. Admissions are relevant and may be proved as against the person who makes them, or his representative in interest; but they cannot be proved by or on behalf of the person who makes them or by his representative in interest, except in the following cases, namely:—

(1) an admission may be proved by or on behalf of the person making it, when it is of such a nature that, if the person making it were dead, it would be relevant as between third persons under section 26;

(2) an admission may be proved by or on behalf of the person making it, when it consists of a statement of the existence of any state of mind or body, relevant or in issue, made at or about the time when such state of mind or body existed, and is accompanied by conduct rendering its falsehood improbable;

(3) an admission may be proved by or on behalf of the person making it, if it is relevant otherwise than as an admission.

Illustrations.

(*a*) The question between A and B is, whether a certain deed is or is not forged. A affirms that it is genuine, B that it is forged.

A may prove a statement by B that the deed is genuine, and B may prove a statement by A that deed is forged; but A cannot prove a statement by himself that the deed is genuine, nor can B prove a statement by himself that the deed is forged.

(*b*) A, the captain of a ship, is tried for casting her away. Evidence is given to show that the ship was taken out of her proper course. A produces a book kept by him in the ordinary course of his business showing observations alleged to have been taken by him from day to day, and indicating that the ship was not taken out of her proper course. A may prove these statements, because they would be admissible between third parties, if he were dead, under clause (*b*) of section 26.

(*c*) A is accused of a crime committed by him at Kolkata. He produces a letter written by himself and dated at Chennai on that day, and bearing the Chennai post-mark of that day. The statement in the date of the letter is admissible, because, if A were dead, it would be admissible under clause (*b*) of section 26.

(*d*) A is accused of receiving stolen goods knowing them to be stolen. He offers to prove that he refused to sell them below their value. A may prove these statements, though they are admissions, because they are explanatory of conduct influenced by facts in issue.

(*e*) A is accused of fraudulently having in his possession counterfeit currency which he knew to be counterfeit. He offers to prove that he asked a skilful person to examine the currency as he doubted whether it was counterfeit or not, and that person did examine it and told him it was genuine. A may prove these facts.

When oral admissions as to contents of documents are relevant.

20. Oral admissions as to the contents of a document are not relevant, unless and until the party proposing to prove them shows that he is entitled to give secondary evidence of the contents of such document under the rules hereinafter contained, or unless the genuineness of a document produced is in question.

Admissions in civil cases when relevant.

21. In civil cases no admission is relevant, if it is made either upon an express condition that evidence of it is not to be given, or under circumstances from which the Court can infer that the parties agreed together that evidence of it should not be given.

Explanation.—Nothing in this section shall be taken to exempt any advocate from giving evidence of any matter of which he may be compelled to give evidence under sub-sections (1) and (2) of section 132.

Confession caused by inducement, threat, coercion or promise, when irrelevant in criminal proceeding.

22. A confession made by an accused person is irrelevant in a criminal proceeding, if the making of the confession appears to the Court to have been caused by any inducement, threat, coercion or promise having reference to the charge against the accused person, proceeding from a person in authority and sufficient, in the opinion of the Court, to give the accused person grounds which would appear to him reasonable for supposing that by making it he would gain any advantage or avoid any evil of a temporal nature in reference to the proceedings against him:

Provided that if the confession is made after the impression caused by any such inducement, threat, coercion or promise has, in the opinion of the Court, been fully removed, it is relevant:

Provided further that if such a confession is otherwise relevant, it does not become irrelevant merely because it was made under a promise of secrecy, or in consequence of a deception practised on the accused person for the purpose of obtaining it, or when he was drunk, or because it was made in answer to questions which he need not have answered, whatever may have been the form of those questions, or because he was not warned that he was not bound to make such confession, and that evidence of it might be given against him.

Confession to police officer.

23. (1) No confession made to a police officer shall be proved as against a person accused of any offence.

(2) No confession made by any person while he is in the custody of a police officer, unless it is made in the immediate presence of a Magistrate shall be proved against him:

Provided that when any fact is deposed to as discovered in consequence of information received from a person accused of any offence, in the custody of a police officer, so much of such information, whether it amounts to a confession or not, as relates distinctly to the fact discovered, may be proved.

Consideration of proved confession affecting person making it and others jointly under trial for same offence.

24. When more persons than one are being tried jointly for the same offence, and a confession made by one of such persons affecting himself and some other of such persons is proved, the Court may take into consideration such confession as against such other person as well as against the person who makes such confession.

Explanation I.—"Offence", as used in this section, includes the abetment of, or attempt to commit, the offence.

Explanation II.—A trial of more persons than one held in the absence of the accused who has absconded or who fails to comply with a proclamation issued under section 84 of the Bharatiya Nagarik Suraksha Sanhita, 2023 shall be deemed to be a joint trial for the purpose of this section.

Illustrations.

(*a*) A and B are jointly tried for the murder of C. It is proved that A said—"B and I murdered C". The Court may consider the effect of this confession as against B.

(*b*) A is on his trial for the murder of C. There is evidence to show that C was murdered by A and B, and that B said—"A and I murdered C". This statement may not be taken into consideration by the Court against A, as B is not being jointly tried.

Admissions not conclusive proof, but may estop.

25. Admissions are not conclusive proof of the matters admitted but they may operate as estoppels under the provisions hereinafter contained.

Statements by persons who cannot be called as witnesses

Cases in which statement of relevant fact by person who is dead or cannot be found, etc., is relevant.

26. Statements, written or verbal, of relevant facts made by a person who is dead, or who cannot be found, or who has become incapable of giving evidence, or whose attendance cannot be procured without an amount of delay or expense which under the circumstances of the case appears to the Court unreasonable, are themselves relevant facts in the following cases, namely:—

(*a*) when the statement is made by a person as to the cause of his death, or as to any of the circumstances of the transaction which resulted in his death, in cases in which the cause of that person's death comes into question. Such statements are relevant whether the person who made them was or was not, at the time when they were made, under expectation of death, and whatever may be the nature of the proceeding in which the cause of his death comes into question;

(*b*) when the statement was made by such person in the ordinary course of business, and in particular when it consists of any entry or memorandum made by him in books kept in the ordinary course of business, or in the discharge of professional duty; or of an acknowledgement written or signed by him of the receipt of money, goods, securities or property of any kind; or of a document used in commerce written or signed by him; or of the date of a letter or other document usually dated, written or signed by him;

(*c*) when the statement is against the pecuniary or proprietary interest of the person making it, or when, if true, it would expose him or would have exposed him to a criminal prosecution or to a suit for damages;

(*d*) when the statement gives the opinion of any such person, as to the existence of any public right or custom or matter of public or general interest, of the existence of which, if it existed, he would have been likely to be aware, and when such statement was made before any controversy as to such right, custom or matter had arisen;

(*e*) when the statement relates to the existence of any relationship by blood, marriage or adoption between persons as to whose relationship by blood, marriage or adoption the person making the statement had special means of knowledge, and when the statement was made before the question in dispute was raised;

(*f*) when the statement relates to the existence of any relationship by blood, marriage or adoption between persons deceased, and is made in any will or deed relating to the affairs of the family to which any such deceased person belonged, or in any family pedigree, or upon any tombstone, family portrait or other thing on which such statements are usually made, and when such statement was made before the question in dispute was raised;

(*g*) when the statement is contained in any deed, will or other document which relates to any such transaction as is specified in clause (*a*) of section 11;

(*h*) when the statement was made by a number of persons, and expressed feelings or impressions on their part relevant to the matter in question.

Illustrations.

(*a*) The question is, whether A was murdered by B; or A dies of injuries received in a transaction in the course of which she was raped. The question is whether she was raped by B; or the question is, whether A was killed by B under such circumstances that a suit would lie against B by A's widow. Statements made by A as to the cause of his or her death, referring respectively to the murder, the rape and the actionable wrong under consideration, are relevant facts.

(*b*) The question is as to the date of A's birth. An entry in the diary of a deceased surgeon regularly kept in the course of business, stating that, on a given day he attended A's mother and delivered her of a son, is a relevant fact.

(*c*) The question is, whether A was in Nagpur on a given day. A statement in the diary of a deceased solicitor, regularly kept in the course of business, that on a given day the solicitor attended A at a place mentioned, in Nagpur, for the purpose of conferring with him upon specified business, is a relevant fact.

(*d*) The question is, whether a ship sailed from Mumbai harbour on a given day. A letter written by a deceased member of a merchant's firm by which she was chartered to their correspondents in Chennai, to whom the cargo was consigned, stating that the ship sailed on a given day from Mumbai port, is a relevant fact.

(*e*) The question is, whether rent was paid to A for certain land. A letter from A's deceased agent to A, saying that he had received the rent on A's account and held it at A's orders is a relevant fact.

(*f*) The question is, whether A and B were legally married. The statement of a deceased clergyman that he married them under such circumstances that the celebration would be a crime is relevant.

(*g*) The question is, whether A, a person who cannot be found, wrote a letter on a certain day. The fact that a letter written by him is dated on that day is relevant.

(*h*) The question is, what was the cause of the wreck of a ship. A protest made by the captain, whose attendance cannot be procured, is a relevant fact.

(*i*) The question is, whether a given road is a public way. A statement by A, a deceased headman of the village, that the road was public, is a relevant fact.

(*j*) The question is, what was the price of grain on a certain day in a particular market. A statement of the price, made by a deceased business person in the ordinary course of his business, is a relevant fact.

(*k*) The question is, whether A, who is dead, was the father of B. A statement by A that B was his son, is a relevant fact.

(*l*) The question is, what was the date of the birth of A. A letter from A's deceased father to a friend, announcing the birth of A on a given day, is a relevant fact.

(*m*) The question is, whether, and when, A and B were married. An entry in a memorandum book by C, the deceased father of B, of his daughter's marriage with A on a given date, is a relevant fact.

(*n*) A sues B for a libel expressed in a painted caricature exposed in a shop window. The question is as to the similarity of the caricature and its libellous character. The remarks of a crowd of spectators on these points may be proved.

Relevancy of certain evidence for proving, in subsequent proceeding, truth of facts therein stated.

27. Evidence given by a witness in a judicial proceeding, or before any person authorised by law to take it, is relevant for the purpose of proving, in a subsequent judicial proceeding, or in a later stage of the same judicial proceeding, the truth of the facts which it states, when the witness is dead or cannot be found, or is incapable of giving evidence, or is kept out of the way by the adverse party, or if his presence cannot be obtained without an amount of delay or expense which, under the circumstances of the case, the Court considers unreasonable:

Provided that the proceeding was between the same parties or their representatives in interest; that the adverse party in the first proceeding had the right and opportunity to cross-examine and the questions in issue were substantially the same in the first as in the second proceeding.

Explanation.—A criminal trial or inquiry shall be deemed to be a proceeding between the prosecutor and the accused within the meaning of this section.

Statements made under special circumstances

Entries in books of account when relevant.

28. Entries in the books of account, including those maintained in an electronic form, regularly kept in the course of business are relevant whenever they refer to a matter into which the Court has to inquire, but such statements shall not alone be sufficient evidence to charge any person with liability.

Illustration.

A sues B for one thousand rupees, and shows entries in his account books showing B to be indebted to him to this amount. The entries are relevant, but are not sufficient, without other evidence, to prove the debt.

Relevancy of entry in public record or an electronic record made in performance of duty.

29. An entry in any public or other official book, register or record or an electronic record, stating a fact in issue or relevant fact, and made by a public servant in the discharge of his official duty, or by any other person in performance of a duty specially enjoined by the law of the country in which such book, register or record or an electronic record, is kept, is itself a relevant fact.

Relevancy of statements in maps, charts and plans.

30. Statements of facts in issue or relevant facts, made in published maps or charts generally offered for public sale, or in maps or plans made under the authority of the Central Government or any State Government, as to matters usually represented or stated in such maps, charts or plans, are themselves relevant facts.

Relevancy of statement as to fact of public nature contained in certain Acts or notifications.

31. When the Court has to form an opinion as to the existence of any fact of a public nature, any statement of it, made in a recital contained in any Central Act or State Act or in a Central Government or State Government notification appearing in the respective Official Gazette or in any printed paper or in electronic or digital form purporting to be such Gazette, is a relevant fact.

Relevancy of statements as to any law contained in law books including electronic or digital form.

32. When the Court has to form an opinion as to a law of any country, any statement of such law contained in a book purporting to be printed or published including in electronic or digital form under the authority of the Government of such country and to contain any such law, and any report of a ruling of the Courts of such country contained in a book including in electronic or digital form purporting to be a report of such rulings, is relevant.

How much of a statement is to be proved

What evidence to be given when statement forms part of a conversation, document, electronic record, book or series of letters or papers.

33. When any statement of which evidence is given forms part of a longer statement, or of a conversation or part of an isolated document, or is contained in a document which forms part of a book, or is contained in part of electronic record or of a connected series of letters or papers, evidence shall be given of so much and no more of the statement, conversation, document, electronic record, book or series of letters or papers as the Court considers necessary in that particular case to the full understanding of the nature and effect of the statement, and of the circumstances under which it was made.

Judgments of Courts when relevant

Previous judgments relevant to bar a second suit or trial.

34. The existence of any judgment, order or decree which by law prevents any Court from taking cognizance of a suit or holding a trial, is a relevant fact when the question is whether such Court ought to take cognizance of such suit or to hold such trial.

Relevancy of certain judgments in probate, etc., jurisdiction.

35. (1) A final judgment, order or decree of a competent Court or Tribunal, in the exercise of probate, matrimonial, admiralty or insolvency jurisdiction, which confers upon or takes away from any person any legal character, or which declares any person to be entitled to any such character, or to be entitled to any specific thing, not as against any specified person but absolutely, is relevant when the existence of any such legal character, or the title of any such person to any such thing, is relevant.

(2) Such judgment, order or decree is conclusive proof that—

    (i) any legal character, which it confers accrued at the time when such judgment, order or decree came into operation;

    (ii) any legal character, to which it declares any such person to be entitled, accrued to that person at the time when such judgment, order or decree declares it to have accrued to that person;

    (iii) any legal character which it takes away from any such person ceased at the time from which such judgment, order or decree declared that it had ceased or should cease; and

    (iv) anything to which it declares any person to be so entitled was the property of that person at the time from which such judgment, order or decree declares that it had been or should be his property.

Relevancy and effect of judgments, orders or decrees, other than those mentioned in section 35.

36. Judgments, orders or decrees other than those mentioned in section 35 are relevant if they relate to matters of a public nature relevant to the enquiry; but such judgments, orders or decrees are not conclusive proof of that which they state.

Illustration.

A sues B for trespass on his land. B alleges the existence of a public right of way over the land, which A denies. The existence of a decree in favour of the defendant, in a suit by A against C for a trespass on the same land, in which C alleged the existence of the same right of way, is relevant, but it is not conclusive proof that the right of way exists.

Judgments, etc., other than those mentioned in sections 34, 35 and 36 when relevant.

37. Judgments or orders or decrees, other than those mentioned in sections 34, 35 and 36, are irrelevant, unless the existence of such judgment, order or decree is a fact in issue, or is relevant under some other provision of this Adhiniyam.

Illustrations.

    (*a*) A and B separately sue C for a libel which reflects upon each of them. C in each case says that the matter alleged to be libellous is true, and the circumstances are such that it is probably true in each case, or in neither. A obtains a decree against C for damages on the ground that C failed to make out his justification. The fact is irrelevant as between B and C.

    (*b*) A prosecutes B for stealing a cow from him. B is convicted. A afterwards sues C for the cow, which B had sold to him before his conviction. As between A and C, the judgment against B is irrelevant.

(*c*) A has obtained a decree for the possession of land against B. C, B's son, murders A in consequence. The existence of the judgment is relevant, as showing motive for a crime.

(*d*) A is charged with theft and with having been previously convicted of theft. The previous conviction is relevant as a fact in issue.

(*e*) A is tried for the murder of B. The fact that B prosecuted A for libel and that A was convicted and sentenced is relevant under section 6 as showing the motive for the fact in issue.

Fraud or collusion in obtaining judgment, or incompetency of Court, may be proved.

38. Any party to a suit or other proceeding may show that any judgment, order or decree which is relevant under section 34, 35 or 36, and which has been proved by the adverse party, was delivered by a Court not competent to deliver it, or was obtained by fraud or collusion.

Opinions of third persons when relevant

Opinions of experts.

39. (1) When the Court has to form an opinion upon a point of foreign law or of science or art, or any other field, or as to identity of handwriting or finger impressions, the opinions upon that point of persons specially skilled in such foreign law, science or art, or any other field, or in questions as to identity of handwriting or finger impressions are relevant facts and such persons are called experts.

Illustrations.

(*a*) The question is, whether the death of A was caused by poison. The opinions of experts as to the symptoms produced by the poison by which A is supposed to have died, are relevant.

(*b*) The question is, whether A, at the time of doing a certain act, was, by reason of unsoundness of mind, incapable of knowing the nature of the act, or that he was doing what was either wrong or contrary to law. The opinions of experts upon the question whether the symptoms exhibited by A commonly show unsoundness of mind, and whether such unsoundness of mind usually renders persons incapable of knowing the nature of the acts which they do, or of knowing that what they do is either wrong or contrary to law, are relevant.

(*c*) The question is, whether a certain document was written by A. Another document is produced which is proved or admitted to have been written by A. The opinions of experts on the question whether the two documents were written by the same person or by different persons, are relevant.

(2) When in a proceeding, the court has to form an opinion on any matter relating to any information transmitted or stored in any computer resource or any other electronic or digital form, the opinion of the Examiner of Electronic Evidence referred to in section 79A of the Information Technology Act, 2000 (21 of 2000), is a relevant fact.

Explanation.—For the purposes of this sub-section, an Examiner of Electronic Evidence shall be an expert.

Facts bearing upon opinions of experts.

40. Facts, not otherwise relevant, are relevant if they support or are inconsistent with the opinions of experts, when such opinions are relevant.

Illustrations.

(*a*) The question is, whether A was poisoned by a certain poison. The fact that other persons, who were poisoned by that poison, exhibited certain symptoms which experts affirm or deny to be the symptoms of that poison, is relevant.

(*b*) The question is, whether an obstruction to a harbour is caused by a certain sea-wall. The fact that other harbours similarly situated in other respects, but where there were no such sea-walls, began to be obstructed at about the same time, is relevant.

Opinion as to handwriting and signature, when relevant.

41. (1) When the Court has to form an opinion as to the person by whom any document was written or signed, the opinion of any person acquainted with the handwriting of the person by whom it is supposed to be written or signed that it was or was not written or signed by that person, is a relevant fact.

Explanation.—A person is said to be acquainted with the handwriting of another person when he has seen that person write, or when he has received documents purporting to be written by that person in answer to documents written by himself or under his authority and addressed to that person, or when, in the ordinary course of business, documents purporting to be written by that person have been habitually submitted to him.

Illustration.

The question is, whether a given letter is in the handwriting of A, a merchant in Itanagar. B is a merchant in Bengaluru, who has written letters addressed to A and received letters purporting to be written by him. C, is B's clerk whose duty it was to examine and file B's correspondence. D is B's broker, to whom B habitually submitted the letters purporting to be written by A for the purpose of advising him thereon. The opinions of B, C and D on the question whether the letter is in the handwriting of A are relevant, though neither B, C nor D ever saw A write.

(2) When the Court has to form an opinion as to the electronic signature of any person, the opinion of the Certifying Authority which has issued the Electronic Signature Certificate is a relevant fact.

Opinion as to existence of general custom or right, when relevant.

42. When the Court has to form an opinion as to the existence of any general custom or right, the opinions, as to the existence of such custom or right, of persons who would be likely to know of its existence if it existed, are relevant.

Explanation.—The expression "general custom or right" includes customs or rights common to any considerable class of persons.

Illustration.

The right of the villagers of a particular village to use the water of a particular well is a general right within the meaning of this section.

Opinion as to usages, tenets, etc., when relevant.

43. When the Court has to form an opinion as to—
    (i) the usages and tenets of any body of men or family;

    (ii) the constitution and governance of any religious or charitable foundation; or

    (iii) the meaning of words or terms used in particular districts or by particular classes of people,

the opinions of persons having special means of knowledge thereon, are relevant facts.

Opinion on relationship, when relevant.

44. When the Court has to form an opinion as to the relationship of one person to another, the opinion, expressed by conduct, as to the existence of such relationship, of any person who, as a member of the family or otherwise, has special means of knowledge on the subject, is a relevant fact:

Provided that such opinion shall not be sufficient to prove a marriage in proceedings under the Divorce Act, 1869 (4 of 1869), or in prosecution under sections 82 and 84 of the Bharatiya Nyaya Sanhita, 2023.

Illustrations.

    (*a*) The question is, whether A and B were married. The fact that they were usually received and treated by their friends as husband and wife, is relevant.

    (*b*) The question is, whether A was the legitimate son of B. The fact that A was always treated as such by members of the family, is relevant.

Grounds of opinion, when relevant.

45. Whenever the opinion of any living person is relevant, the grounds on which such opinion is based are also relevant.

Illustration.

An expert may give an account of experiments performed by him for the purpose of forming his opinion.

Character when relevant

In civil cases character to prove conduct imputed, irrelevant.

46. In civil cases the fact that the character of any person concerned is such as to render probable or improbable any conduct imputed to him, is irrelevant, except in so far as such character appears from facts otherwise relevant.

In criminal cases previous good character relevant.

47. In criminal proceedings the fact that the person accused is of a good character, is relevant.

Evidence of character or previous sexual experience not relevant in certain cases.

48. In a prosecution for an offence under section 64, section 65, section 66, section 67, section 68, section 69, section 70, section 71, section 74, section 75, section 76, section 77 or section 78 of the Bharatiya Nyaya Sanhita, 2023 or for attempt to commit any such offence, where the question of consent is in issue, evidence of the character of the victim or of such person's previous sexual experience with any person shall not be relevant on the issue of such consent or the quality of consent.

Previous bad character not relevant, except in reply.

49. In criminal proceedings, the fact that the accused has a bad character, is irrelevant, unless evidence has been given that he has a good character, in which case it becomes relevant.

Explanation 1.—This section does not apply to cases in which the bad character of any person is itself a fact in issue.

Explanation 2.—A previous conviction is relevant as evidence of bad character.

Character as affecting damages.

50. In civil cases, the fact that the character of any person is such as to affect the amount of damages which he ought to receive, is relevant.

Explanation.—In this section and sections 46, 47 and 49, the word "character" includes both reputation and disposition; but, except as provided in section 49, evidence may be given only of general reputation and general disposition, and not of particular acts by which reputation or disposition has been shown.

PART III

ON PROOF

Chapter III

FACTS WHICH NEED NOT BE PROVED

Fact judicially noticeable need not be proved.

51. No fact of which the Court will take judicial notice need be proved.

Facts of which Court shall take judicial notice.

52. (1) The Court shall take judicial notice of the following facts, namely:—

(*a*) all laws in force in the territory of India including laws having extra-territorial operation;

(*b*) international treaty, agreement or convention with country or countries by India, or decisions made by India at international associations or other bodies;

(*c*) the course of proceeding of the Constituent Assembly of India, of Parliament of India and of the State Legislatures;

(*d*) the seals of all Courts and Tribunals;

(*e*) the seals of Courts of Admiralty and Maritime Jurisdiction, Notaries Public, and all seals which any person is authorised to use by the Constitution, or by an Act of Parliament or State Legislatures, or Regulations having the force of law in India;

(*f*) the accession to office, names, titles, functions, and signatures of the persons filling for the time being any public office in any State, if the fact of their appointment to such office is notified in any Official Gazette;

(*g*) the existence, title and national flag of every country or sovereign recognised by the Government of India;

(*h*) the divisions of time, the geographical divisions of the world, and public festivals, fasts and holidays notified in the Official Gazette;

(*i*) the territory of India;

(*j*) the commencement, continuance and termination of hostilities between the Government of India and any other country or body of persons;

(*k*) the names of the members and officers of the Court and of their deputies and subordinate officers and assistants, and also of all officers acting in execution of its process, and of advocates and other persons authorised by law to appear or act before it;

(*l*) the rule of the road on land or at sea.

(2) In the cases referred to in sub-section (1) and also on all matters of public history, literature, science or art, the Court may resort for its aid to appropriate books or documents of reference and if the Court is called upon by any person to take judicial notice of any fact, it may refuse to do so unless and until such person produces any such book or document as it may consider necessary to enable it to do so.

Facts admitted need not be proved.

53. No fact needs to be proved in any proceeding which the parties thereto or their agents agree to admit at the hearing, or which, before the hearing, they agree to admit by any writing under their hands, or which by any rule of pleading in force at the time they are deemed to have admitted by their pleadings:

Provided that the Court may, in its discretion, require the facts admitted to be proved otherwise than by such admissions.

Chapter IV

OF ORAL EVIDENCE

Proof of facts by oral evidence.

54. All facts, except the contents of documents may be proved by oral evidence.

Oral evidence to be direct.

55. Oral evidence shall, in all cases whatever, be direct; if it refers to,—

(i) a fact which could be seen, it must be the evidence of a witness who says he saw it;

(ii) a fact which could be heard, it must be the evidence of a witness who says he heard it;

(iii) a fact which could be perceived by any other sense or in any other manner, it must be the evidence of a witness who says he perceived it by that sense or in that manner;

(iv) an opinion or to the grounds on which that opinion is held, it must be the evidence of the person who holds that opinion on those grounds:

Provided that the opinions of experts expressed in any treatise commonly offered for sale, and the grounds on which such opinions are held, may be proved by the production of such treatises if the author is dead or cannot be found, or has become incapable of giving evidence, or cannot be called as a witness without an amount of delay or expense which the Court regards as unreasonable:

Provided further that, if oral evidence refers to the existence or condition of any material thing other than a document, the Court may, if it thinks fit, require the production of such material thing for its inspection.

Chapter V

OF DOCUMENTARY EVIDENCE

Proof of contents of documents.

56. The contents of documents may be proved either by primary or by secondary evidence.

Primary evidence.

57. Primary evidence means the document itself produced for the inspection of the Court.

Explanation 1.—Where a document is executed in several parts, each part is primary evidence of the document.

Explanation 2.—Where a document is executed in counterpart, each counterpart being executed by one or some of the parties only, each counterpart is primary evidence as against the parties executing it.

Explanation 3.—Where a number of documents are all made by one uniform process, as in the case of printing, lithography or photography, each is primary evidence of the contents of the rest; but, where they are all copies of a common original, they are not primary evidence of the contents of the original.

Explanation 4.—Where an electronic or digital record is created or stored, and such storage occurs simultaneously or sequentially in multiple files, each such file is primary evidence.

Explanation 5.—Where an electronic or digital record is produced from proper custody, such electronic and digital record is primary evidence unless it is disputed.

Explanation 6.—Where a video recording is simultaneously stored in electronic form and transmitted or broadcast or transferred to another, each of the stored recordings is primary evidence.

Explanation 7.—Where an electronic or digital record is stored in multiple storage spaces in a computer resource, each such automated storage, including temporary files, is primary evidence.

Illustration.

A person is shown to have been in possession of a number of placards, all printed at one time from one original. Any one of the placards is primary evidence of the contents of any other, but no one of them is primary evidence of the contents of the original.

Secondary evidence.

58. Secondary evidence includes—
  (i)   certified copies given under the provisions hereinafter contained;
  (ii) copies made from the original by mechanical processes which in themselves ensure the accuracy of the copy, and copies compared with such copies;
  (iii) copies made from or compared with the original;
  (iv) counterparts of documents as against the parties who did not execute them;
  (v)   oral accounts of the contents of a document given by some person who has himself seen it;

  (vi) oral admissions;

  (vii) written admissions;

(viii) evidence of a person who has examined a document, the original of which consists of numerous accounts or other documents which cannot conveniently be examined in Court, and who is skilled in the examination of such documents.

Illustrations.

(*a*) A photograph of an original is secondary evidence of its contents, though the two have not been compared, if it is proved that the thing photographed was the original.

(*b*) A copy compared with a copy of a letter made by a copying machine is secondary evidence of the contents of the letter, if it is shown that the copy made by the copying machine was made from the original.

(*c*) A copy transcribed from a copy, but afterwards compared with the original, is secondary evidence; but the copy not so compared is not secondary evidence of the original, although the copy from which it was transcribed was compared with the original.

(*d*) Neither an oral account of a copy compared with the original, nor an oral account of a photograph or machine-copy of the original, is secondary evidence of the original.

Proof of documents by primary evidence.

59. Documents shall be proved by primary evidence except in the cases hereinafter mentioned.

Cases in which secondary evidence relating to documents may be given.

60. Secondary evidence may be given of the existence, condition, or contents of a document in the following cases, namely:—

(*a*) when the original is shown or appears to be in the possession or power—

  (i) of the person against whom the document is sought to be proved; or

  (ii) of any person out of reach of, or not subject to, the process of the Court; or

(iii)   of any person legally bound to produce it,

and when, after the notice mentioned in section 64 such person does not produce it;

(*b*) when the existence, condition or contents of the original have been proved to be admitted in writing by the person against whom it is proved or by his representative in interest;

(*c*) when the original has been destroyed or lost, or when the party offering evidence of its contents cannot, for any other reason not arising from his own default or neglect, produce it in reasonable time;

(*d*) when the original is of such a nature as not to be easily movable;

(*e*) when the original is a public document within the meaning of section 74;

(*f*) when the original is a document of which a certified copy is permitted by this Adhiniyam, or by any other law in force in India to be given in evidence;

(*g*) when the originals consist of numerous accounts or other documents which cannot conveniently be examined in Court, and the fact to be proved is the general result of the whole collection.

Explanation.—For the purposes of—

(i)   clauses (*a*), (*c*) and (*d*), any secondary evidence of the contents of the document is admissible;

(ii)   clause (*b*), the written admission is admissible;

(iii)   clause (*e*) or (*f*), a certified copy of the document, but no other kind of secondary evidence, is admissible;

(iv)   clause (*g*), evidence may be given as to the general result of the documents by any person who has examined them, and who is skilled in the examination of such document.

Electronic or digital record.

61. Nothing in this Adhiniyam shall apply to deny the admissibility of an electronic or digital record in the evidence on the ground that it is an electronic or digital record and such record shall, subject to section 63, have the same legal effect, validity and enforceability as other document.

Special provisions as to evidence relating to electronic record.

62. The contents of electronic records may be proved in accordance with the provisions of section 63.

Admissibility of electronic records.

63. (1) Notwithstanding anything contained in this Adhiniyam, any information contained in an electronic record which is printed on paper, stored, recorded or copied in optical or magnetic media or semiconductor memory which is produced by a computer or any communication device or otherwise stored, recorded or copied in any electronic form (hereinafter referred to as the computer output) shall be deemed to be also a document, if the conditions mentioned in this section are satisfied in relation to the information and computer in question and shall be admissible in any proceedings, without further proof or production of the original, as evidence or any contents of the original or of any fact stated therein of which direct evidence would be admissible.

(2) The conditions referred to in sub-section (*1*) in respect of a computer output shall be the following, namely:—

    (*a*) the computer output containing the information was produced by the computer or communication device during the period over which the computer or communication device was used regularly to create, store or process information for the purposes of any activity regularly carried on over that period by the person having lawful control over the use of the computer or communication device;

    (*b*) during the said period, information of the kind contained in the electronic record or of the kind from which the information so contained is derived was regularly fed into the computer or communication device in the ordinary course of the said activities;

    (*c*) throughout the material part of the said period, the computer or communication device was operating properly or, if not, then in respect of any period in which it was not operating properly or was out of operation during that part of the period, was not such as to affect the electronic record or the accuracy of its contents; and

    (*d*) the information contained in the electronic record reproduces or is derived from such information fed into the computer or communication device in the ordinary course of the said activities.

(3) Where over any period, the function of creating, storing or processing information for the purposes of any activity regularly carried on over that period as mentioned in clause (*a*) of sub-section (2) was regularly performed by means of one or more computers or communication device, whether—

(*a*) in standalone mode; or

(*b*) on a computer system; or

(*c*) on a computer network; or

(*d*) on a computer resource enabling information creation or providing information processing and storage; or

(*e*) through an intermediary,

all the computers or communication devices used for that purpose during that period shall be treated for the purposes of this section as constituting a single computer or communication device; and references in this section to a computer or communication device shall be construed accordingly.

(4) In any proceeding where it is desired to give a statement in evidence by virtue of this section, a certificate doing any of the following things shall be submitted along with the electronic record at each instance where it is being submitted for admission, namely:—

(*a*) identifying the electronic record containing the statement and describing the manner in which it was produced;

(*b*) giving such particulars of any device involved in the production of that electronic record as may be appropriate for the purpose of showing that the electronic record was produced by a computer or a communication device referred to in clauses (*a*) to (*e*) of sub-section (3);

(*c*) dealing with any of the matters to which the conditions mentioned in sub-section (2) relate,

and purporting to be signed by a person in charge of the computer or communication device or the management of the relevant activities (whichever is appropriate) and an expert shall be evidence of any matter stated in the certificate; and for the purposes of this sub-section it shall be sufficient for a matter to be stated to the best of the knowledge and belief of the person stating it in the certificate specified in the Schedule.

(5) For the purposes of this section,—

(*a*) information shall be taken to be supplied to a computer or communication device if it is supplied thereto in any appropriate form and whether it is so supplied directly or (with or without human intervention) by means of any appropriate equipment;

(*b*) a computer output shall be taken to have been produced by a computer or communication device whether it was produced by it directly or (with or without human intervention) by means of any appropriate equipment or by other electronic means as referred to in clauses (*a*) to (*e*) of sub-section (3).

Rules as to notice to produce.

64. Secondary evidence of the contents of the documents referred to in clause (*a*) of section 60, shall not be given unless the party proposing to give such secondary evidence has previously given to the party in whose possession or power the document is, or to his advocate or representative, such notice to produce it as is prescribed by law; and if no notice is prescribed by law, then such notice as the Court considers reasonable under the circumstances of the case:

Provided that such notice shall not be required in order to render secondary evidence admissible in any of the following cases, or in any other case in which the Court thinks fit to dispense with it:—

(*a*) when the document to be proved is itself a notice;

(*b*) when, from the nature of the case, the adverse party must know that he will be required to produce it;

(*c*) when it appears or is proved that the adverse party has obtained possession of the original by fraud or force;

(*d*) when the adverse party or his agent has the original in Court;

(*e*) when the adverse party or his agent has admitted the loss of the document;

(*f*) when the person in possession of the document is out of reach of, or not subject to, the process of the Court.

Proof of signature and handwriting of person alleged to have signed or written document produced.

65. If a document is alleged to be signed or to have been written wholly or in part by any person, the signature or the handwriting of so much of the document as is alleged to be in that person's handwriting must be proved to be in his handwriting.

Proof as to electronic signature.

66. Except in the case of a secure electronic signature, if the electronic signature of any subscriber is alleged to have been affixed to an electronic record, the fact that such electronic signature is the electronic signature of the subscriber must be proved.

Proof of execution of document required by law to be attested.

67. If a document is required by law to be attested, it shall not be used as evidence until one attesting witness at least has been called for the purpose of proving its execution, if there be an attesting witness alive, and subject to the process of the Court and capable of giving evidence:

Provided that it shall not be necessary to call an attesting witness in proof of the execution of any document, not being a will, which has been registered in accordance with the provisions of the Indian Registration Act, 1908 (16 of 1908), unless its execution by the person by whom it purports to have been executed is specifically denied.

Proof where no attesting witness found.

68. If no such attesting witness can be found, it must be proved that the attestation of one attesting witness at least is in his handwriting, and that the signature of the person executing the document is in the handwriting of that person.

Admission of execution by party to attested document.

69. The admission of a party to an attested document of its execution by himself shall be sufficient proof of its execution as against him, though it be a document required by law to be attested.

Proof when attesting witness denies execution.

70. If the attesting witness denies or does not recollect the execution of the document, its execution may be proved by other evidence.

Proof of document not required by law to be attested.

71. An attested document not required by law to be attested may be proved as if it was unattested.

Comparison of signature, writing or seal with others admitted or proved.

72. (1) In order to ascertain whether a signature, writing or seal is that of the person by whom it purports to have been written or made, any signature, writing, or seal admitted or proved to the satisfaction of the Court to have been written or made by that person may be compared with the one which is to be proved, although that signature, writing or seal has not been produced or proved for any other purpose.

(2) The Court may direct any person present in Court to write any words or figures for the purpose of enabling the Court to compare the words or figures so written with any words or figures alleged to have been written by such person.

(3) This section applies also, with any necessary modifications, to finger impressions.

Proof as to verification of digital signature.

73. In order to ascertain whether a digital signature is that of the person by whom it purports to have been affixed, the Court may direct—
    (*a*) that person or the Controller or the Certifying Authority to produce the Digital Signature Certificate;
    (*b*) any other person to apply the public key listed in the Digital Signature Certificate and verify the digital signature purported to have been affixed by that person.

Public documents

Public and private documents.

74. (1) The following documents are public documents:—
    (*a*) documents forming the acts, or records of the acts—
        (i)   of the sovereign authority;
        (ii)   of official bodies and tribunals; and
        (iii)   of public officers, legislative, judicial and executive of India or of a foreign country;

(*b*) public records kept in any State or Union territory of private documents.

(2) All other documents except the documents referred to in sub-section (1) are private.

Certified copies of public documents.

75. Every public officer having the custody of a public document, which any person has a right to inspect, shall give that person on demand a copy of it on payment of the legal fees therefor, together with a certificate written at the foot of such copy that it is a true copy of such document or part thereof, as the case may be, and such certificate shall be dated and subscribed by such officer with his name and his official title, and shall be sealed, whenever such officer is authorised by law to make use of a seal; and such copies so certified shall be called certified copies.

Explanation.—Any officer who, by the ordinary course of official duty, is authorised to deliver such copies, shall be deemed to have the custody of such documents within the meaning of this section.

Proof of documents by production of certified copies.

76. Such certified copies may be produced in proof of the contents of the public documents or parts of the public documents of which they purport to be copies.

Proof of other official documents.

77. The following public documents may be proved as follows:—
  (*a*) Acts, orders or notifications of the Central Government in any of its Ministries and Departments or of any State Government or any Department of any State Government or Union territory Administration—
   (i) by the records of the Departments, certified by the head of those Departments respectively; or
   (ii) by any document purporting to be printed by order of any such Government;
  (*b*) the proceedings of Parliament or a State Legislature, by the journals of those bodies respectively, or by published Acts or abstracts, or by copies purporting to be printed by order of the Government concerned;

(*c*) proclamations, orders or Regulations issued by the President of India or the Governor of a State or the Administrator or Lieutenant Governor of a Union territory, by copies or extracts contained in the Official Gazette;

(*d*) the Acts of the Executive or the proceedings of the Legislature of a foreign country, by journals published by their authority, or commonly received in that country as such, or by a copy certified under the seal of the country or sovereign, or by a recognition thereof in any Central Act;

(*e*) the proceedings of a municipal or local body in a State, by a copy of such proceedings, certified by the legal keeper thereof, or by a printed book purporting to be published by the authority of such body;

(*f*) public documents of any other class in a foreign country, by the original or by a copy certified by the legal keeper thereof, with a certificate under the seal of a Notary Public, or of an Indian Consul or diplomatic agent, that the copy is duly certified by the officer having the legal custody of the original, and upon proof of the character of the document according to the law of the foreign country.

Presumptions as to documents

Presumption as to genuineness of certified copies.

78. (1) The Court shall presume to be genuine every document purporting to be a certificate, certified copy or other document, which is by law declared to be admissible as evidence of any particular fact and which purports to be duly certified by any officer of the Central Government or of a State Government:

Provided that such document is substantially in the form and purports to be executed in the manner directed by law in that behalf.

(2) The Court shall also presume that any officer by whom any such document purports to be signed or certified, held, when he signed it, the official character which he claims in such paper.

Presumption as to documents produced as record of evidence, etc.

79. Whenever any document is produced before any Court, purporting to be a record or memorandum of the evidence, or of any part of the evidence, given by a witness in a judicial proceeding or before any officer authorised by law to take such evidence or to be a statement or confession by any prisoner or accused person, taken in accordance with law, and purporting to be signed by any Judge or Magistrate, or by any such officer as aforesaid, the Court shall presume that—

(i) the document is genuine;

(ii) any statements as to the circumstances under which it was taken, purporting to be made by the person signing it, are true; and

(iii) such evidence, statement or confession was duly taken.

Presumption as to Gazettes, newspapers, and other documents.

80. The Court shall presume the genuineness of every document purporting to be the Official Gazette, or to be a newspaper or journal, and of every document purporting to be a document directed by any law to be kept by any person, if such document is kept substantially in the form required by law and is produced from proper custody.

Explanation.—For the purposes of this section and section 92, document is said to be in proper custody if it is in the place in which, and looked after by the person with whom such document is required to be kept; but no custody is improper if it is proved to have had a legitimate origin, or if the circumstances of the particular case are such as to render that origin probable.

Presumption as to Gazettes in electronic or digital record.

81. The Court shall presume the genuineness of every electronic or digital record purporting to be the Official Gazette, or purporting to be electronic or digital record directed by any law to be kept by any person, if such electronic or digital record is kept substantially in the form required by law and is produced from proper custody.

Explanation.—For the purposes of this section and section 93 electronic records are said to be in proper custody if they are in the place in which, and looked after by the person with whom such document is required to be kept; but no custody is improper if it is proved to have had a legitimate origin, or the circumstances of the particular case are such as to render that origin probable.

Presumption as to maps or plans made by authority of Government.

82. The Court shall presume that maps or plans purporting to be made by the authority of the Central Government or any State Government were so made, and are accurate; but maps or plans made for the purposes of any cause must be proved to be accurate.

Presumption as to collections of laws and reports of decisions.

83. The Court shall presume the genuineness of, every book purporting to be printed or published under the authority of the Government of any country, and to contain any of the laws of that country, and of every book purporting to contain reports of decisions of the Courts of such country.

Presumption as to powers-of-attorney.

84. The Court shall presume that every document purporting to be a power-of-attorney, and to have been executed before, and authenticated by, a Notary Public, or any Court, Judge, Magistrate, Indian Consul or Vice-Consul, or representative of the Central Government, was so executed and authenticated.

Presumption as to electronic agreements.

85. The Court shall presume that every electronic record purporting to be an agreement containing the electronic or digital signature of the parties was so concluded by affixing the electronic or digital signature of the parties.

Presumption as to electronic records and electronic signatures.

86. (1) In any proceeding involving a secure electronic record, the Court shall presume unless contrary is proved, that the secure electronic record has not been altered since the specific point of time to which the secure status relates.

(2) In any proceeding, involving secure electronic signature, the Court shall presume unless the contrary is proved that—

    (*a*) the secure electronic signature is affixed by subscriber with the intention of signing or approving the electronic record;

    (*b*) except in the case of a secure electronic record or a secure electronic signature, nothing in this section shall create any presumption, relating to authenticity and integrity of the electronic record or any electronic signature.

Presumption as to Electronic Signature Certificates.

87. The Court shall presume, unless contrary is proved, that the information listed in an Electronic Signature Certificate is correct, except for information specified as subscriber information which has not been verified, if the certificate was accepted by the subscriber.

Presumption as to certified copies of foreign judicial records.

88. (1) The Court may presume that any document purporting to be a certified copy of any judicial record of any country beyond India is genuine and accurate, if the document purports to be certified in any manner which is certified by any representative of the Central Government in or for such country to be the manner commonly in use in that country for the certification of copies of judicial records.

(2) An officer who, with respect to any territory or place outside India is a Political Agent therefor, as defined in clause (43) of section 3 of the General Clauses Act, 1897 (10 of 1897), shall, for the purposes of this section, be deemed to be a representative of the Central Government in and for the country comprising that territory or place.

Presumption as to books, maps and charts.

89. The Court may presume that any book to which it may refer for information on matters of public or general interest, and that any published map or chart, the statements of which are relevant facts, and which is produced for its inspection, was written and published by the person, and at the time and place, by whom or at which it purports to have been written or published.

Presumption as to electronic messages.

90. The Court may presume that an electronic message, forwarded by the originator through an electronic mail server to the addressee to whom the message purports to be addressed corresponds with the message as fed into his computer for transmission; but the Court shall not make any presumption as to the person by whom such message was sent.

Presumption as to due execution, etc., of documents not produced.

91. The Court shall presume that every document, called for and not produced after notice to produce, was attested, stamped and executed in the manner required by law.

Presumption as to documents thirty years old.

92. Where any document, purporting or proved to be thirty years old, is produced from any custody which the Court in the particular case considers proper, the Court may presume that the signature and every other part of such document, which purports to be in the handwriting of any particular person, is in that person's handwriting, and, in the case of a document executed or attested, that it was duly executed and attested by the persons by whom it purports to be executed and attested.

Explanation.—The *Explanation* to section 80 shall also apply to this section.

Illustrations.

    (*a*) A has been in possession of landed property for a long time. He produces from his custody deeds relating to the land showing his titles to it. The custody shall be proper.

    (*b*) A produces deeds relating to landed property of which he is the mortgagee. The mortgagor is in possession. The custody shall be proper.

    (*c*) A, a connection of B, produces deeds relating to lands in B's possession, which were deposited with him by B for safe custody. The custody shall be proper.

Presumption as to electronic records five years old.

93. Where any electronic record, purporting or proved to be five years old, is produced from any custody which the Court in the particular case considers proper, the Court may presume that the electronic signature which purports to be the electronic signature of any particular person was so affixed by him or any person authorised by him in this behalf.

Explanation.—The *Explanation* to section 81 shall also apply to this section.

CHAPTER VI

OF THE EXCLUSION OF ORAL EVIDENCE BY DOCUMENTARY EVIDENCE

Evidence of terms of contracts, grants and other dispositions of property reduced to form of document.

94. When the terms of a contract, or of a grant, or of any other disposition of property, have been reduced to the form of a document, and in all cases in which any matter is required by law to be reduced to the form of a document, no evidence shall be given in proof of the terms of such contract, grant or other disposition of property, or of such matter, except the document itself, or secondary evidence of its contents in cases in which secondary evidence is admissible under the provisions hereinbefore contained.

Exception 1.—When a public officer is required by law to be appointed in writing, and when it is shown that any particular person has acted as such officer, the writing by which he is appointed need not be proved.

Exception 2.—Wills admitted to probate in India may be proved by the probate.

Explanation 1.—This section applies equally to cases in which the contracts, grants or dispositions of property referred to are contained in one document, and to cases in which they are contained in more documents than one.

Explanation 2.—Where there are more originals than one, one original only need be proved.

Explanation 3.—The statement, in any document whatever, of a fact other than the facts referred to in this section, shall not preclude the admission of oral evidence as to the same fact.

Illustrations.

(*a*) If a contract be contained in several letters, all the letters in which it is contained must be proved.

(*b*) If a contract is contained in a bill of exchange, the bill of exchange must be proved.

(*c*) If a bill of exchange is drawn in a set of three, one only need be proved.

(*d*) A contracts, in writing, with B, for the delivery of indigo upon certain terms. The contract mentions the fact that B had paid A the price of other indigo contracted for verbally on another occasion. Oral evidence is offered that no payment was made for the other indigo. The evidence is admissible.

(*e*) A gives B a receipt for money paid by B. Oral evidence is offered of the payment. The evidence is admissible.

Exclusion of evidence of oral agreement.

95. When the terms of any such contract, grant or other disposition of property, or any matter required by law to be reduced to the form of a document, have been proved according to section 94, no evidence of any oral agreement or statement shall be admitted, as between the parties to any such instrument or their representatives in interest, for the purpose of contradicting, varying, adding to, or subtracting from, its terms:

Provided that any fact may be proved which would invalidate any document, or which would entitle any person to any decree or order relating thereto; such as fraud, intimidation, illegality, want of due execution, want of capacity in any contracting party, want or failure of consideration, or mistake in fact or law:

Provided further that the existence of any separate oral agreement as to any matter on which a document is silent, and which is not inconsistent with its terms, may be proved. In considering whether or not this proviso applies, the Court shall have regard to the degree of formality of the document:

Provided also that the existence of any separate oral agreement, constituting a condition precedent to the attaching of any obligation under any such contract, grant or disposition of property, may be proved:

Provided also that the existence of any distinct subsequent oral agreement to rescind or modify any such contract, grant or disposition of property, may be proved, except in cases in which such contract, grant or disposition of property is by law required to be in writing, or has been registered according to the law in force for the time being as to the registration of documents:

Provided also that any usage or custom by which incidents not expressly mentioned in any contract are usually annexed to contracts of that description, may be proved:

Provided also that the annexing of such incident would not be repugnant to, or inconsistent with, the express terms of the contract:

Provided also that any fact may be proved which shows in what manner the language of a document is related to existing facts.

Illustrations.

(*a*) A policy of insurance is effected on goods "in ships from Kolkata to Visakhapatnam". The goods are shipped in a particular ship which is lost. The fact that particular ship was orally excepted from the policy, cannot be proved.

(*b*) A agrees absolutely in writing to pay B one thousand rupees on the 1st March, 2023. The fact that, at the same time, an oral agreement was made that the money should not be paid till the 31st March, 2023, cannot be proved.

(*c*) An estate called "the Rampur tea estate" is sold by a deed which contains a map of the property sold. The fact that land not included in the map had always been regarded as part of the estate and was meant to pass by the deed cannot be proved.

(*d*) A enters into a written contract with B to work certain mines, the property of B, upon certain terms. A was induced to do so by a misrepresentation of B's as to their value. This fact may be proved.

(*e*) A institutes a suit against B for the specific performance of a contract, and also prays that the contract may be reformed as to one of its provisions, as that provision was inserted in it by mistake. A may prove that such a mistake was made as would by law entitle him to have the contract reformed.

(*f*) A orders goods of B by a letter in which nothing is said as to the time of payment, and accepts the goods on delivery. B sues A for the price. A may show that the goods were supplied on credit for a term still unexpired.

(*g*) A sells B a horse and verbally warrants him sound. A gives B a paper in these words—"Bought of A a horse for thirty thousand rupees". B may prove the verbal warranty.

(*h*) A hires lodgings of B, and gives B a card on which is written—"Rooms, ten thousand rupees a month". A may prove a verbal agreement that these terms were to include partial board. A hires lodging of B for a year, and a regularly stamped agreement, drawn up by an advocate, is made between them. It is silent on the subject of board. A may not prove that board was included in the term verbally.

(*i*) A applies to B for a debt due to A by sending a receipt for the money. B keeps the receipt and does not send the money. In a suit for the amount, A may prove this.

(*j*) A and B make a contract in writing to take effect upon the happening of a certain contingency. The writing is left with B who sues A upon it. A may show the circumstances under which it was delivered.

Exclusion of evidence to explain or amend ambiguous document.

96. When the language used in a document is, on its face, ambiguous or defective, evidence may not be given of facts which would show its meaning or supply its defects.

Illustrations.

(*a*) A agrees, in writing, to sell a horse to B for "one lakh rupees or one lakh fifty thousand rupees". Evidence cannot be given to show which price was to be given.

(*b*) A deed contains blanks. Evidence cannot be given of facts which would show how they were meant to be filled.

Exclusion of evidence against application of document to existing facts.

97. When language used in a document is plain in itself, and when it applies accurately to existing facts, evidence may not be given to show that it was not meant to apply to such facts.

Illustration.

A sells to B, by deed, "my estate at Rampur containing one hundred *bighas*". A has an estate at Rampur containing one hundred *bighas*. Evidence may not be given of the fact that the estate meant to be sold was one situated at a different place and of a different size.

Evidence as to document unmeaning in reference to existing facts.

98. When language used in a document is plain in itself, but is unmeaning in reference to existing facts, evidence may be given to show that it was used in a peculiar sense.

Illustration.

A sells to B, by deed, "my house in Kolkata". A had no house in Kolkata, but it appears that he had a house at Howrah, of which B had been in possession since the execution of the deed. These facts may be proved to show that the deed related to the house at Howrah.

Evidence as to application of language which can apply to one only of several persons.

99. When the facts are such that the language used might have been meant to apply to any one, and could not have been meant to apply to more than one, of several persons or things, evidence may be given of facts which show which of those persons or things it was intended to apply to.

Illustrations.

(*a*) A agrees to sell to B, for one thousand rupees, "my white horse". A has two white horses. Evidence may be given of facts which show which of them was meant.

(*b*) A agrees to accompany B to Ramgarh. Evidence may be given of facts showing whether Ramgarh in Rajasthan or Ramgarh in Uttarakhand was meant.

Evidence as to application of language to one of two sets of facts, to neither of which the whole correctly applies.

100. When the language used applies partly to one set of existing facts, and partly to another set of existing facts, but the whole of it does not apply correctly to either, evidence may be given to show to which of the two it was meant to apply.

Illustration.

A agrees to sell to B "my land at X in the occupation of Y". A has land at X, but not in the occupation of Y, and he has land in the occupation of Y but it is not at X. Evidence may be given of facts showing which he meant to sell.

Evidence as to meaning of illegible characters, etc.

101. Evidence may be given to show the meaning of illegible or not commonly intelligible characters, of foreign, obsolete, technical, local and regional expressions, of abbreviations and of words used in a peculiar sense.

Illustration.

A, sculptor, agrees to sell to B, "all my mods". A has both models and modelling tools.

Who may give evidence of agreement varying terms of document.

102. Persons who are not parties to a document, or their representatives in interest, may give evidence of any facts tending to show a contemporaneous agreement varying the terms of the document.

Illustration.

A and B make a contract in writing that B shall sell A certain cotton, to be paid for on delivery. At the same time, they make an oral agreement that three months' credit shall be given to A. This could not be shown as between A and B, but it might be shown by C, if it affected his interests.

Saving of provisions of Indian Succession Act relating to wills.

103. Nothing in this Chapter shall be taken to affect any of the provisions of the Indian Succession Act, 1925 (39 of 1925) as to the construction of wills.

PART IV

PRODUCTION AND EFFECT OF EVIDENCE

Chapter VII

OF THE BURDEN OF PROOF

Burden of proof.

104. Whoever desires any Court to give judgment as to any legal right or liability dependent on the existence of facts which he asserts must prove that those facts exist, and when a person is bound to prove the existence of any fact, it is said that the burden of proof lies on that person.

Illustrations.

(*a*) A desires a Court to give judgment that B shall be punished for a crime which A says B has committed. A must prove that B has committed the crime.

(*b*) A desires a Court to give judgment that he is entitled to certain land in the possession of B, by reason of facts which he asserts, and which B denies, to be true. A must prove the existence of those facts.

On whom burden of proof lies.

105. The burden of proof in a suit or proceeding lies on that person who would fail if no evidence at all were given on either side.

Illustrations.

(*a*) A sues B for land of which B is in possession, and which, as A asserts, was left to A by the will of C, B's father. If no evidence were given on either side, B would be entitled to retain his possession. Therefore, the burden of proof is on A.

(*b*) A sues B for money due on a bond. The execution of the bond is admitted, but B says that it was obtained by fraud, which A denies. If no evidence were given on either side, A would succeed, as the bond is not disputed and the fraud is not proved. Therefore, the burden of proof is on B.

Burden of proof as to particular fact.

106. The burden of proof as to any particular fact lies on that person who wishes the Court to believe in its existence, unless it is provided by any law that the proof of that fact shall lie on any particular person.

Illustration.

A prosecutes B for theft, and wishes the Court to believe that B admitted the theft to C. A must prove the admission. B wishes the Court to believe that, at the time in question, he was elsewhere. He must prove it.

Burden of proving fact to be proved to make evidence admissible.

107. The burden of proving any fact necessary to be proved in order to enable any person to give evidence of any other fact is on the person who wishes to give such evidence.

Illustrations.

(*a*) A wishes to prove a dying declaration by B. A must prove B's death.

(*b*) A wishes to prove, by secondary evidence, the contents of a lost document. A must prove that the document has been lost.

Burden of proving that case of accused comes within exceptions.

108. When a person is accused of any offence, the burden of proving the existence of circumstances bringing the case within any of the General Exceptions in the Bharatiya Nyaya Sanhita, 2023 or within any special exception or proviso contained in any other part of the said Sanhita, or in any law defining the offence, is upon him, and the Court shall presume the absence of such circumstances.

Illustrations.

(*a*) A, accused of murder, alleges that, by reason of unsoundness of mind, he did not know the nature of the act. The burden of proof is on A.

(*b*) A, accused of murder, alleges that, by grave and sudden provocation, he was deprived of the power of self-control. The burden of proof is on A.

(*c*) Section 117 of the Bharatiya Nyaya Sanhita, 2023 provides that whoever, except in the case provided for by sub-section (2) of section 122, voluntarily causes grievous hurt, shall be subject to certain punishments. A is charged with voluntarily causing grievous hurt under section 117. The burden of proving the circumstances bringing the case under sub-section (2) of section 122 lies on A.

Burden of proving fact especially within knowledge.

109. When any fact is especially within the knowledge of any person, the burden of proving that fact is upon him.

Illustrations.

(*a*) When a person does an act with some intention other than that which the character and circumstances of the act suggest, the burden of proving that intention is upon him.

(*b*) A is charged with travelling on a railway without a ticket. The burden of proving that he had a ticket is on him.

Burden of proving death of person known to have been alive within thirty years.

110. When the question is whether a man is alive or dead, and it is shown that he was alive within thirty years, the burden of proving that he is dead is on the person who affirms it.

Burden of proving that person is alive who has not been heard of for seven years.

111. When the question is whether a man is alive or dead, and it is proved that he has not been heard of for seven years by those who would naturally have heard of him if he had been alive, the burden of proving that he is alive is shifted to the person who affirms it.

Burden of proof as to relationship in the cases of partners, landlord and tenant, principal and agent.

112. When the question is whether persons are partners, landlord and tenant, or principal and agent, and it has been shown that they have been acting as such, the burden of proving that they do not stand, or have ceased to stand, to each other in those relationships respectively, is on the person who affirms it.

Burden of proof as to ownership.

113. When the question is whether any person is owner of anything of which he is shown to be in possession, the burden of proving that he is not the owner is on the person who affirms that he is not the owner.

Proof of good faith in transactions where one party is in relation of active confidence.

114. Where there is a question as to the good faith of a transaction between parties, one of whom stands to the other in a position of active confidence, the burden of proving the good faith of the transaction is on the party who is in a position of active confidence.

Illustrations.

(*a*) The good faith of a sale by a client to an advocate is in question in a suit brought by the client. The burden of proving the good faith of the transaction is on the advocate.

(*b*) The good faith of a sale by a son just come of age to a father is in question in a suit brought by the son. The burden of proving the good faith of the transaction is on the father.

Presumption as to certain offences.

115. (1) Where a person is accused of having committed any offence specified in sub-section (2), in—

(*a*) any area declared to be a disturbed area under any enactment for the time being in force, making provision for the suppression of disorder and restoration and maintenance of public order; or

(*b*) any area in which there has been, over a period of more than one month, extensive disturbance of the public peace,

and it is shown that such person had been at a place in such area at a time when firearms or explosives were used at or from that place to attack or resist the members of any armed forces or the forces charged with the maintenance of public order acting in the discharge of their duties, it shall be presumed, unless the contrary is shown, that such person had committed such offence.

(2) The offences referred to in sub-section (1) are the following, namely:—

    (*a*) an offence under section 147, section 148, section 149 or section 150 of the Bharatiya Nyaya Sanhita, 2023;

    (*b*) criminal conspiracy or attempt to commit, or abetment of, an offence under section 149 or section 150 of the Bharatiya Nyaya Sanhita, 2023.

Birth during marriage, conclusive proof of legitimacy.

116. The fact that any person was born during the continuance of a valid marriage between his mother and any man, or within two hundred and eighty days after its dissolution, the mother remaining unmarried, shall be conclusive proof that he is the legitimate child of that man, unless it can be shown that the parties to the marriage had no access to each other at any time when he could have been begotten.

Presumption as to abetment of suicide by a married woman.

117. When the question is whether the commission of suicide by a woman had been abetted by her husband or any relative of her husband and it is shown that she had committed suicide within a period of seven years from the date of her marriage and that her husband or such relative of her husband had subjected her to cruelty, the Court may presume, having regard to all the other circumstances of the case, that such suicide had been abetted by her husband or by such relative of her husband.

Explanation.—For the purposes of this section, "cruelty" shall have the same meaning as in section 86 of the Bharatiya Nyaya Sanhita, 2023.

Presumption as to dowry death.

118. When the question is whether a person has committed the dowry death of a woman and it is shown that soon before her death, such woman had been subjected by such person to cruelty or harassment for, or in connection with, any demand for dowry, the Court shall presume that such person had caused the dowry death.

Explanation.—For the purposes of this section, "dowry death" shall have the same meaning as in section 80 of the Bharatiya Nyaya Sanhita, 2023.

Court may presume existence of certain facts.

119. (1) The Court may presume the existence of any fact which it thinks likely to have happened, regard being had to the common course of natural events, human conduct and public and private business, in their relation to the facts of the particular case.

Illustrations.

The Court may presume that—
>   (*a*) a man who is in possession of stolen goods soon, after the theft is either the thief or has received the goods knowing them to be stolen, unless he can account for his possession;
>   (*b*) an accomplice is unworthy of credit, unless he is corroborated in material particulars;
>   (*c*) a bill of exchange, accepted or endorsed, was accepted or endorsed for good consideration;
>   (*d*) a thing or state of things which has been shown to be in existence within a period shorter than that within which such things or state of things usually cease to exist, is still in existence;
>   (*e*) judicial and official acts have been regularly performed;
>   (*f*) the common course of business has been followed in particular cases;
>   (*g*) evidence which could be and is not produced would, if produced, be unfavourable to the person who withholds it;
>   (*h*) if a man refuses to answer a question which he is not compelled to answer by law, the answer, if given, would be unfavourable to him;
>   (*i*) when a document creating an obligation is in the hands of the obligor, the obligation has been discharged.

(2) The Court shall also have regard to such facts as the following, in considering whether such maxims do or do not apply to the particular case before it:—
>   (i) as to *Illustration* (*a*)—a shop-keeper has in his bill a marked rupee soon after it was stolen, and cannot account for its possession specifically, but is continually receiving rupees in the course of his business;
>   (ii) as to *Illustration* (*b*)—A, a person of the highest character, is tried

for causing a man's death by an act of negligence in arranging certain machinery. B, a person of equally good character, who also took part in the arrangement, describes precisely what was done, and admits and explains the common carelessness of A and himself;

(iii) as to *Illustration* (*b*)—a crime is committed by several persons. A, B and C, three of the criminals, are captured on the spot and kept apart from each other. Each gives an account of the crime implicating D, and the accounts corroborate each other in such a manner as to render previous concert highly improbable;

(iv) as to *Illustration* (*c*)—A, the drawer of a bill of exchange, was a man of business. B, the acceptor, was a young and ignorant person, completely under A's influence;

(v) as to *Illustration* (*d*)—it is proved that a river ran in a certain course five years ago, but it is known that there have been floods since that time which might change its course;

(vi) as to *Illustration* (*e*)—a judicial act, the regularity of which is in question, was performed under exceptional circumstances;

(vii) as to *Illustration* (*f*)—the question is, whether a letter was received. It is shown to have been posted, but the usual course of the post was interrupted by disturbances;

(viii) as to *Illustration* (*g*)—a man refuses to produce a document which would bear on a contract of small importance on which he is sued, but which might also injure the feelings and reputation of his family;

(ix) as to *Illustration* (*h*)—a man refuses to answer a question which he is not compelled by law to answer, but the answer to it might cause loss to him in matters unconnected with the matter in relation to which it is asked;

(x) as to *Illustration* (*i*)—a bond is in possession of the obligor, but the circumstances of the case are such that he may have stolen it.

Presumption as to absence of consent in certain prosecution for rape.

120. In a prosecution for rape under sub-section (2) of section 64 of the Bharatiya Nyaya Sanhita, 2023, where sexual intercourse by the accused is proved and the question is whether it was without the consent of the woman alleged to have been raped and such woman states in her evidence before the Court that she did not consent, the Court shall presume that she did not consent.

Explanation.—In this section, "sexual intercourse" shall mean any of the acts mentioned in section 63 of the Bharatiya Nyaya Sanhita, 2023.

Chapter VIII

ESTOPPEL

Estoppel.

121. When one person has, by his declaration, act or omission, intentionally caused or permitted another person to believe a thing to be true and to act upon such belief, neither he nor his representative shall be allowed, in any suit or proceeding between himself and such person or his representative, to deny the truth of that thing.

Illustration.

A intentionally and falsely leads B to believe that certain land belongs to A, and thereby induces B to buy and pay for it. The land afterwards becomes the property of A, and A seeks to set aside the sale on the ground that, at the time of the sale, he had no title. He must not be allowed to prove his want of title.

Estoppel of tenant and of licensee of person in possession.

122. No tenant of immovable property, or person claiming through such tenant, shall, during the continuance of the tenancy or any time thereafter, be permitted to deny that the landlord of such tenant had, at the beginning of the tenancy, a title to such immovable property; and no person who came upon any immovable property by the licence of the person in possession thereof shall be permitted to deny that such person had a title to such possession at the time when such licence was given.

Estoppel of acceptor of bill of exchange, bailee or licensee.

123. No acceptor of a bill of exchange shall be permitted to deny that the drawer had authority to draw such bill or to endorse it; nor shall any bailee or licensee be permitted to deny that his bailor or licensor had, at the time when the bailment or licence commenced, authority to make such bailment or grant such licence.

Explanation 1.—The acceptor of a bill of exchange may deny that the bill was really drawn by the person by whom it purports to have been drawn.

Explanation 2.—If a bailee delivers the goods bailed to a person other than the bailor, he may prove that such person had a right to them as against the bailor.

Chapter IX

OF WITNESSES

Who may testify.

124. All persons shall be competent to testify unless the Court considers that they are prevented from understanding the questions put to them, or from giving rational answers to those questions, by tender years, extreme old age, disease, whether of body or mind, or any other cause of the same kind.

Explanation.—A person of unsound mind is not incompetent to testify, unless he is prevented by his unsoundness of mind from understanding the questions put to him and giving rational answers to them.

Witness unable to communicate verbally.

125. A witness who is unable to speak may give his evidence in any other manner in which he can make it intelligible, as by writing or by signs; but such writing must be written and the signs made in open Court and evidence so given shall be deemed to be oral evidence:

Provided that if the witness is unable to communicate verbally, the Court shall take the assistance of an interpreter or a special educator in recording the statement, and such statement shall be videographed.

Competency of husband and wife as witnesses in certain cases.

126. (1) In all civil proceedings the parties to the suit, and the husband or wife of any party to the suit, shall be competent witnesses.

(2) In criminal proceedings against any person, the husband or wife of such person, respectively, shall be a competent witness.

Judges and Magistrates.

127. No Judge or Magistrate shall, except upon the special order of some Court to which he is subordinate, be compelled to answer any question as to his own conduct in Court as such Judge or Magistrate, or as to anything which came to his knowledge in Court as such Judge or Magistrate; but he may be examined as to other matters which occurred in his presence whilst he was so acting.

Illustrations.

(*a*) A, on his trial before the Court of Session, says that a deposition was improperly taken by B, the Magistrate. B cannot be compelled to answer questions as to this, except upon the special order of a superior Court.

(*b*) A is accused before the Court of Session of having given false evidence before B, a Magistrate. B cannot be asked what A said, except upon the special order of the superior Court.

(*c*) A is accused before the Court of Session of attempting to murder a police officer whilst on his trial before B, a Sessions Judge. B may be examined as to what occurred.

Communications during marriage.

128. No person who is or has been married, shall be compelled to disclose any communication made to him during marriage by any person to whom he is or has been married; nor shall he be permitted to disclose any such communication, unless the person who made it, or his representative in interest, consents, except in suits between married persons, or proceedings in which one married person is prosecuted for any crime committed against the other.

Evidence as to affairs of State.

129. No one shall be permitted to give any evidence derived from unpublished official records relating to any affairs of State, except with the permission of the officer at the head of the department concerned, who shall give or withhold such permission as he thinks fit.

Official communications.

130. No public officer shall be compelled to disclose communications made to him in official confidence, when he considers that the public interests would suffer by the disclosure.

Information as to commission of offences.

131. No Magistrate or police officer shall be compelled to say when he got any information as to the commission of any offence, and no revenue officer shall be compelled to say when he got any information as to the commission of any offence against the public revenue.

Explanation.—"revenue officer" means any officer employed in or about the business of any branch of the public revenue.

Professional communications.

132. (1) No advocate, shall at any time be permitted, unless with his client's express consent, to disclose any communication made to him in the course and for the purpose of his service as such advocate, by or on behalf of his client, or to state the contents or condition of any document with which he has become acquainted in the course and for the purpose of his professional service, or to disclose any advice given by him to his client in the course and for the purpose of such service:

Provided that nothing in this section shall protect from disclosure of—
    (*a*) any such communication made in furtherance of any illegal purpose;
    (*b*) any fact observed by any advocate, in the course of his service as such, showing that any crime or fraud has been committed since the commencement of his service.

(2) It is immaterial whether the attention of such advocate referred to in the proviso to sub-section (1), was or was not directed to such fact by or on behalf of his client.

Explanation.—The obligation stated in this section continues after the professional service has ceased.

Illustrations.

(*a*) A, a client, says to B, an advocate—"I have committed forgery, and I wish you to defend me". As the defence of a man known to be guilty is not a criminal purpose, this communication is protected from disclosure.

(*b*) A, a client, says to B, an advocate—"I wish to obtain possession of property by the use of a forged deed on which I request you to sue". This communication, being made in furtherance of a criminal purpose, is not protected from disclosure.

(*c*) A, being charged with embezzlement, retains B, an advocate, to defend him. In the course of the proceedings, B observes that an entry has been made in A's account book, charging A with the sum said to have been embezzled, which entry was not in the book at the commencement of his professional service. This being a fact observed by B in the course of his service, showing that a fraud has been committed since the commencement of the proceedings, it is not protected from disclosure.

(3) The provisions of this section shall apply to interpreters, and the clerks or employees of advocates.

Privilege not waived by volunteering evidence.

133. If any party to a suit gives evidence therein at his own instance or otherwise, he shall not be deemed to have consented thereby to such disclosure as is mentioned in section 132; and, if any party to a suit or proceeding calls any such advocate, as a witness, he shall be deemed to have consented to such disclosure only if he questions such advocate, on matters which, but for such question, he would not be at liberty to disclose.

Confidential communication with legal advisers.

134. No one shall be compelled to disclose to the Court any confidential communication which has taken place between him and his legal adviser, unless he offers himself as a witness, in which case he may be compelled to disclose any such communications as may appear to the Court necessary to be known in order to explain any evidence which he has given, but no others.

Production of title-deeds of witness not a party.

135. No witness who is not a party to a suit shall be compelled to produce his title-deeds to any property, or any document in virtue of which he holds any property as pledgee or mortgagee or any document the production of which might tend to criminate him, unless he has agreed in writing to produce them with the person seeking the production of such deeds or some person through whom he claims.

Production of documents or electronic records which another person, having possession, could refuse to produce.

136. No one shall be compelled to produce documents in his possession or electronic records under his control, which any other person would be entitled to refuse to produce if they were in his possession or control, unless such last-mentioned person consents to their production.

Witness not excused from answering on ground that answer will criminate.

137. A witness shall not be excused from answering any question as to any matter relevant to the matter in issue in any suit or in any civil or criminal proceeding, upon the ground that the answer to such question will criminate, or may tend directly or indirectly to criminate, such witness, or that it will expose, or tend directly or indirectly to expose, such witness to a penalty or forfeiture of any kind:

Provided that no such answer, which a witness shall be compelled to give, shall subject him to any arrest or prosecution, or be proved against him in any criminal proceeding, except a prosecution forgiving false evidence by such answer.

Accomplice.

138. An accomplice shall be a competent witness against an accused person; and a conviction is not illegal if it proceeds upon the corroborated testimony of an accomplice.

Number of witnesses.

139. No particular number of witnesses shall in any case be required for the proof of any fact.

Chapter X

OF EXAMINATION OF WITNESSES

Order of production and examination of witnesses.

140. The order in which witnesses are produced and examined shall be regulated by the law and practice for the time being relating to civil and criminal procedure respectively, and, in the absence of any such law, by the discretion of the Court.

Judge to decide as to admissibility of evidence.

141. (1) When either party proposes to give evidence of any fact, the Judge may ask the party proposing to give the evidence in what manner the alleged fact, if proved, would be relevant; and the Judge shall admit the evidence if he thinks that the fact, if proved, would be relevant, and not otherwise.

(2) If the fact proposed to be proved is one of which evidence is admissible only upon proof of some other fact, such last mentioned fact must be proved before evidence is given of the fact first mentioned, unless the party undertakes to give proof of such fact, and the Court is satisfied with such undertaking.

(3) If the relevancy of one alleged fact depends upon another alleged fact being first proved, the Judge may, in his discretion, either permit evidence of the first fact to be given before the second fact is proved, or require evidence to be given of the second fact before evidence is given of the first fact.

Illustrations.

(*a*) It is proposed to prove a statement about a relevant fact by a person alleged to be dead, which statement is relevant under section 26. The fact that the person is dead must be proved by the person proposing to prove the statement, before evidence is given of the statement.

(*b*) It is proposed to prove, by a copy, the contents of a document said to be lost. The fact that the original is lost must be proved by the person proposing to produce the copy, before the copy is produced.

(*c*) A is accused of receiving stolen property knowing it to have been stolen. It is proposed to prove that he denied the possession of the property. The relevancy of the denial depends on the identity of the property. The Court may, in its discretion, either require the property to be identified before the denial of the possession is proved, or permit the denial of the possession to be proved before the property is identified.

(*d*) It is proposed to prove a fact A which is said to have been the cause or effect of a fact in issue. There are several intermediate facts B, C and D which must be shown to exist before the fact A can be regarded as the cause or effect of the fact in issue. The Court may either permit A to be proved before B, C or D is proved, or may require proof of B, C and D before permitting proof of A.

Examination of witnesses.

142. (1) The examination of a witness by the party who calls him shall be called his examination-in-chief.

(2) The examination of a witness by the adverse party shall be called his cross-examination.

(3) The examination of a witness, subsequent to the cross-examination, by the party who called him, shall be called his re-examination.

Order of examinations.

143. (1) Witnesses shall be first examined-in-chief, then (if the adverse party so desires) cross-examined, then (if the party calling him so desires) re-examined.

(2) The examination-in-chief and cross-examination must relate to relevant facts, but the cross-examination need not be confined to the facts to which the witness testified on his examination-in-chief.

(3) The re-examination shall be directed to the explanation of matters referred to in cross-examination; and, if new matter is, by permission of the Court, introduced in re-examination, the adverse party may further cross-examine upon that matter.

Cross-examination of person called to produce a document.

144. A person summoned to produce a document does not become a witness by the mere fact that he produces it, and cannot be cross-examined unless and until he is called as a witness.

Witnesses to character.

145. Witnesses to character may be cross-examined and re-examined.

Leading questions.

146. (1) Any question suggesting the answer which the person putting it wishes or expects to receive, is called a leading question.

(2) Leading questions must not, if objected to by the adverse party, be asked in an examination-in-chief, or in a re-examination, except with the permission of the Court.

(3) The Court shall permit leading questions as to matters which are introductory or undisputed, or which have, in its opinion, been already sufficiently proved.

(4) Leading questions may be asked in cross-examination.

Evidence as to matters in writing.

147. Any witness may be asked, while under examination, whether any contract, grant or other disposition of property, as to which he is giving evidence, was not contained in a document, and if he says that it was, or if he is about to make any statement as to the contents of any document, which, in the opinion of the Court, ought to be produced, the adverse party may object to such evidence being given until such document is produced, or until facts have been proved which entitle the party who called the witness to give secondary evidence of it.

Explanation.—A witness may give oral evidence of statements made by other persons about the contents of documents if such statements are in themselves relevant facts.

Illustration.

The question is, whether A assaulted B. C deposes that he heard A say to D—"B wrote a letter accusing me of theft, and I will be revenged on him". This statement is relevant, as showing A's motive for the assault, and evidence may be given of it, though no other evidence is given about the letter.

Cross-examination as to previous statements in writing.

148. A witness may be cross-examined as to previous statements made by him in writing or reduced into writing, and relevant to matters in question, without such writing being shown to him, or being proved; but, if it is intended to contradict him by the writing, his attention must, before the writing can be proved, be called to those parts of it which are to be used for the purpose of contradicting him.

Questions lawful in cross-examination.

149. When a witness is cross-examined, he may, in addition to the questions hereinbefore referred to, be asked any questions which tend—
  (*a*) to test his veracity; or
  (*b*) to discover who he is and what is his position in life; or
  (*c*) to shake his credit, by injuring his character, although the answer to such questions might tend directly or indirectly to criminate him, or might expose or tend directly or indirectly to expose him to a penalty or forfeiture:

Provided that in a prosecution for an offence under section 64, section 65, section 66, section 67, section 68, section 69, section 70 or section 71 of the Bharatiya Nyaya Sanhita, 2023 or for attempt to commit any such offence, where the question of consent is an issue, it shall not be permissible to adduce evidence or to put questions in the cross-examination of the victim as to the general immoral character, or previous sexual experience, of such victim with any person for proving such consent or the quality of consent.

When witness to be compelled to answer.

150. If any such question relates to a matter relevant to the suit or proceeding, the provisions of section 137 shall apply thereto.

Court to decide when question shall be asked and when witness compelled to answer.

151. (1) If any such question relates to a matter not relevant to the suit or proceeding, except in so far as it affects the credit of the witness by injuring his character, the Court shall decide whether or not the witness shall be compelled to answer it, and may, if it thinks fit, warn the witness that he is not obliged to answer it.

(2) In exercising its discretion, the Court shall have regard to the following considerations, namely:—

(*a*) such questions are proper if they are of such a nature that the truth of the imputation conveyed by them would seriously affect the opinion of the Court as to the credibility of the witness on the matter to which he testifies;

(*b*) such questions are improper if the imputation which they convey relates to matters so remote in time, or of such a character, that the truth of the imputation would not affect, or would affect in a slight degree, the opinion of the Court as to the credibility of the witness on the matter to which he testifies;

(*c*) such questions are improper if there is a great disproportion between the importance of the imputation made against the witness's character and the importance of his evidence;

(*d*) the Court may, if it sees fit, draw, from the witness's refusal to answer, the inference that the answer if given would be unfavourable.

Question not to be asked without reasonable grounds.

152. No such question as is referred to in section 151 ought to be asked, unless the person asking it has reasonable grounds for thinking that the imputation which it conveys is well-founded.

Illustrations.

(*a*) An advocate is instructed by another advocate that an important witness is a dacoit. This is a reasonable ground for asking the witness whether he is a dacoit.

(*b*) An advocate is informed by a person in Court that an important witness is a dacoit. The informant, on being questioned by the advocate, gives satisfactory reasons for his statement. This is a reasonable ground for asking the witness whether he is a dacoit.

(*c*) A witness, of whom nothing whatever is known, is asked at random whether he is a dacoit. There are here no reasonable grounds for the question.

(*d*) A witness, of whom nothing whatever is known, being questioned as to his mode of life and means of living, gives unsatisfactory answers. This may be a reasonable ground for asking him if he is a dacoit.

Procedure of Court in case of question being asked without reasonable grounds.

153. If the Court is of opinion that any such question was asked without reasonable grounds, it may, if it was asked by any advocate, report the circumstances of the case to the High Court or other authority to which such advocate is subject in the exercise of his profession.

Indecent and scandalous questions.

154. The Court may forbid any questions or inquiries which it regards as indecent or scandalous, although such questions or inquiries may have some bearing on the questions before the Court, unless they relate to facts in issue, or to matters necessary to be known in order to determine whether or not the facts in issue existed.

Questions intended to insult or annoy.

155. The Court shall forbid any question which appears to it to be intended to insult or annoy, or which, though proper in itself, appears to the Court needlessly offensive in form.

Exclusion of evidence to contradict answers to questions testing veracity.

156. When a witness has been asked and has answered any question which is relevant to the inquiry only in so far as it tends to shake his credit by injuring his character, no evidence shall be given to contradict him; but, if he answers falsely, he may afterwards be charged with giving false evidence.

Exception 1.—If a witness is asked whether he has been previously convicted of any crime and denies it, evidence may be given of his previous conviction.

Exception 2.—If a witness is asked any question tending to impeach his impartiality, and answers it by denying the facts suggested, he may be contradicted.

Illustrations.

(*a*) A claim against an underwriter is resisted on the ground of fraud. The claimant is asked whether, in a former transaction, he had not made a fraudulent claim. He denies it. Evidence is offered to show that he did make such a claim. The evidence is inadmissible.

(*b*) A witness is asked whether he was not dismissed from a situation for dishonesty. He denies it. Evidence is offered to show that he was dismissed for dishonesty. The evidence is not admissible.

(*c*) A affirms that on a certain day he saw B at Goa. A is asked whether he himself was not on that day at Varanasi. He denies it. Evidence is offered to show that A was on that day at Varanasi. The evidence is admissible, not as contradicting A on a fact which affects his credit, but as contradicting the alleged fact that B was seen on the day in question in Goa. In each of these cases, the witness might, if his denial was false, be charged with giving false evidence.

(*d*) A is asked whether his family has not had a blood feud with the family of B against whom he gives evidence. He denies it. He may be contradicted on the ground that the question tends to impeach his impartiality.

Question by party to his own witness.

157. (1) The Court may, in its discretion, permit the person who calls a witness to put any question to him which might be put in cross-examination by the adverse party.

(2) Nothing in this section shall disentitle the person so permitted under sub-section (1), to rely on any part of the evidence of such witness.

Impeaching credit of witness.

158. The credit of a witness may be impeached in the following ways by the adverse party, or, with the consent of the Court, by the party who calls him—

(*a*) by the evidence of persons who testify that they, from their knowledge of the witness, believe him to be unworthy of credit;

(*b*) by proof that the witness has been bribed, or has accepted the offer of a bribe, or has received any other corrupt inducement to give his evidence;

(*c*) by proof of former statements inconsistent with any part of his evidence which is liable to be contradicted.

Explanation.—A witness declaring another witness to be unworthy of credit may not, upon his examination-in-chief, give reasons for his belief, but he may be asked his reasons in cross-examination, and the answers which he gives cannot be contradicted, though, if they are false, he may afterwards be charged with giving false evidence.

Illustrations.

(*a*) A sues B for the price of goods sold and delivered to B. C says that he delivered the goods to B. Evidence is offered to show that, on a previous occasion, he said that he had not delivered goods to B. The evidence is admissible.

(*b*) A is accused of the murder of B. C says that B, when dying, declared that A had given B the wound of which he died. Evidence is offered to show that, on a previous occasion, C said that B, when dying, did not declare that A had given B the wound of which he died. The evidence is admissible.

Questions tending to corroborate evidence of relevant fact, admissible.

159. When a witness whom it is intended to corroborate gives evidence of any relevant fact, he may be questioned as to any other circumstances which he observed at or near to the time or place at which such relevant fact occurred, if the Court is of opinion that such circumstances, if proved, would corroborate the testimony of the witness as to the relevant fact which he testifies.

Illustration.

A, an accomplice, gives an account of a robbery in which he took part. He describes various incidents unconnected with the robbery which occurred on his way to and from the place where it was committed. Independent evidence of these facts may be given in order to corroborate his evidence as to the robbery itself.

Former statements of witness may be proved to corroborate later testimony as to same fact.

160. In order to corroborate the testimony of a witness, any former statement made by such witness relating to the same fact, at or about the time when the fact took place, or before any authority legally competent to investigate the fact, may be proved.

What matters may be proved in connection with proved statement relevant under section 26 or 27.

161. Whenever any statement, relevant under section 26 or 27, is proved, all matters may be proved either in order to contradict or to corroborate it, or in order to impeach or confirm the credit of the person by whom it was made, which might have been proved if that person had been called as a witness and had denied upon cross-examination the truth of the matter suggested.

Refreshing memory.

162. (1) A witness may, while under examination, refresh his memory by referring to any writing made by himself at the time of the transaction concerning which he is questioned, or so soon afterwards that the Court considers it likely that the transaction was at that time fresh in his memory:

Provided that the witness may also refer to any such writing made by any other person, and read by the witness within the time aforesaid, if when he read it, he knew it to be correct.

(2) Whenever a witness may refresh his memory by reference to any document, he may, with the permission of the Court, refer to a copy of such document:

Provided that the Court be satisfied that there is sufficient reason for the non-production of the original:

Provided further that an expert may refresh his memory by reference to professional treatises.

Testimony to facts stated in document mentioned in section 162.

163. A witness may also testify to facts mentioned in any such document as is mentioned in section 162, although he has no specific recollection of the facts themselves, if he is sure that the facts were correctly recorded in the document.

Illustration.

A book-keeper may testify to facts recorded by him in books regularly kept in the course of business, if he knows that the books were correctly kept, although he has forgotten the particular transactions entered.

Right of adverse party as to writing used to refresh memory.

164. Any writing referred to under the provisions of the two last preceding sections shall be produced and shown to the adverse party if he requires it; such party may, if he pleases, cross-examine the witness thereupon.

Production of documents.

165. (1) A witness summoned to produce a document shall, if it is in his possession or power, bring it to Court, notwithstanding any objection which there may be to its production or to its admissibility:

Provided that the validity of any such objection shall be decided on by the Court.

(2) The Court, if it sees fit, may inspect the document, unless it refers to matters of State, or take other evidence to enable it to determine on its admissibility.

(3) If for such a purpose it is necessary to cause any document to be translated, the Court may, if it thinks fit, direct the translator to keep the contents secret, unless the document is to be given in evidence and, if the interpreter disobeys such direction, he shall be held to have committed an offence under section 198 of the Bharatiya Nyaya Sanhita, 2023:

Provided that no Court shall require any communication between the Ministers and the President of India to be produced before it.

Giving, as evidence, of document called for and produced on notice.

166. When a party calls for a document which he has given the other party notice to produce, and such document is produced and inspected by the party calling for its production, he is bound to give it as evidence if the party producing it requires him to do so.

Using, as evidence, of document production of which was refused on notice.

167. When a party refuses to produce a document which he has had notice to produce, he cannot afterwards use the document as evidence without the consent of the other party or the order of the Court.

Illustration.

A sues B on an agreement and gives B notice to produce it. At the trial, A calls for the document and B refuses to produce it. A gives secondary evidence of its contents. B seeks to produce the document itself to contradict the secondary evidence given by A, or in order to show that the agreement is not stamped. He cannot do so.

Judge's power to put questions or order production.

168. The Judge may, in order to discover or obtain proof of relevant facts, ask any question he considers necessary, in any form, at any time, of any witness, or of the parties about any fact; and may order the production of any document or thing; and neither the parties nor their representatives shall be entitled to make any objection to any such question or order, nor, without the leave of the Court, to cross-examine any witness upon any answer given in reply to any such question:

Provided that the judgment must be based upon facts declared by this Adhiniyam to be relevant, and duly proved:

Provided further that this section shall not authorise any Judge to compel any witness to answer any question, or to produce any document which such witness would be entitled to refuse to answer or produce under sections 127 to 136, both inclusive, if the question were asked or the document were called for by the adverse party; nor shall the Judge ask any question which it would be improper for any other person to ask under section 151 or 152; nor shall he dispense with primary evidence of any document, except in the cases hereinbefore excepted.

Chapter XI

OF IMPROPER ADMISSION AND
REJECTION OF EVIDENCE

No new trial for improper admission or rejection of evidence.

169. The improper admission or rejection of evidence shall not be ground of itself for a new trial or reversal of any decision in any case, if it shall appear to the Court before which such objection is raised that, independently of the evidence objected to and admitted, there was sufficient evidence to justify the decision, or that, if the rejected evidence had been received, it ought not to have varied the decision.

Chapter XII

REPEAL AND SAVINGS

Repeal and savings.

170. (1) The Indian Evidence Act, 1872 (1 of 1872) is hereby repealed.

(2) Notwithstanding such repeal, if, immediately before the date on which this Adhiniyam comes into force, there is any application, trial, inquiry, investigation, proceeding or appeal pending, then, such application, trial, inquiry, investigation, proceeding or appeal shall be dealt with under the provisions of the Indian Evidence Act, 1872 (1 of 1872), as in force immediately before such commencement, as if this Adhiniyam had not come into force.

THE SCHEDULE

[*See* section 63(4)(*c*)]

CERTIFICATE

PART A

(To be filled by the Party)

I, _______________ (Name), Son/daughter/spouse of _______________ residing/employed at _______________________________ do hereby solemnly affirm and sincerely state and submit as follows:—

I have produced electronic record/output of the digital record taken from the following device/digital record source (tick mark):—

Computer / Storage Media □   DVR □   Mobile □

Flash Drive □   CD/DVD □   Server □

Cloud □   Other □

Other: _______________________________

Make & Model: _______________   Color: _______________

Serial Number: _______________

IMEI/UIN/UID/MAC/Cloud ID _______________ (as applicable) and any other relevant information, if any, about the device/digital record _______________ (specify).

The digital device or the digital record source was under the lawful control for regularly creating, storing or processing information for the purposes of carrying out regular activities and during this period, the computer or the communication device was working properly and the relevant information was regularly fed into the computer during the ordinary course of business. If the computer/digital device at any point of time was not working properly or out of operation, then it has not affected the electronic/digital record or its accuracy. The digital device or the source of the digital record is:—

Owned □   Maintained □   Managed □   Operated □

by me (select as applicable).

I state that the HASH value/s of the electronic/digital record/s is _______________, obtained through the following algorithm:—

☐ SHA1:
☐ SHA256:
☐ MD5:
☐ Other_______________ (Legally acceptable standard)
(Hash report to be enclosed with the certificate)

(Name and signature)

Date (DD/MM/YYYY): _______
Time (IST): _______ hours (In 24 hours format)
Place: _______________

PART B

(To be filled by the Expert)

I, _______________ (Name), Son/daughter/spouse of _______________ residing/employed at _______________ do hereby solemnly affirm and sincerely state and submit as follows:—

The produced electronic record/output of the digital record are obtained from the following device/digital record source (tick mark):—

Computer / Storage Media ☐   DVR ☐   Mobile ☐

Flash Drive ☐   CD/DVD ☐   Server ☐

Cloud ☐   Other ☐

Other: _______________________________

Make & Model: _______________   Color: _______________

Serial Number: _______________

IMEI/UIN/UID/MAC/Cloud ID _______________ (as applicable) and any other relevant information, if any, about the device/digital record _______________ (specify).

I state that the HASH value/s of the electronic/digital record/s is _______________, obtained through the following algorithm:—

☐ SHA1:
☐ SHA256:
☐ MD5:
☐ Other_______________ (Legally acceptable standard)

(Hash report to be enclosed with the certificate)

(Name and signature)

Date (DD/MM/YYYY): _______
Time (IST): _____ hours (In 24 hours format)
Place: _____________

DIWAKAR SINGH,
Joint Secretary & Legislative Counsel to the Govt. of India.

COMPARISON BETWEEN INDIAN EVIDENCE ACT, 1872 AND BHARATIYA SAKSHYA ADHINIYAM, 2023

INDIAN EVIDENCE ACT, 1872	BHARATIYA SAKSHYA ADHINIYAM, 2023
PART I **CHAPTER I** **PRELIMINARY**	**PART I** **RELEVANCY OF FACTS** **CHAPTER I** **PRELIMINARY**
1. Short title. Extent. Commencement of Act.	1. Short title, application and commencement.
2. Repealed	
3. Interpretation-clause. **(Definition of "India" - Deleted)** 4. —May Presume. —Shall presume. —Conclusive proof.	2. **Definitions. (Change)**
CHAPTER II. **OF THE RELEVANCY OF** **FACTS**	**PART II** **CHAPTER II** **RELEVANCY OF FACTS**
5. Evidence may be given of facts in issue and relevant facts.	3. Evidence may be given of facts in issue and relevant facts.
	Closely connected facts
6. Relevancy of facts forming part of same transaction.	4. **Relevancy of facts forming part of same transaction. (Change)**
7. Facts which are the occasion, cause or effect of facts in issue.	5. Facts which are occasion, cause or effect of facts in issue or relevant facts.
8. Motive, preparation and previous or subsequent conduct.	6. Motive, preparation and previous or subsequent conduct.
9. Facts necessary to explain or introduce relevant facts.	7. Facts necessary to explain or introduce fact in issue or relevant facts.
10. Things said or done by conspirator in reference to common design.	8. Things said or done by conspirator in reference to common design.

INDIAN EVIDENCE ACT, 1872	BHARATIYA SAKSHYA ADHINIYAM, 2023
11. When facts not otherwise relevant become relevant.	9. When facts not otherwise relevant become relevant.
12. In suits for damages, facts tending to enable Court to determine amount are relevant.	10. Facts tending to enable Court to determine amount are relevant in suits for damages.
13. Facts relevant when right or custom is in question.	11. Facts relevant when right or custom is in question.
14. Facts showing existence of state of mind, or of body of bodily feeling.	12. Facts showing existence of state of mind, or of body or bodily feeling.
15. Facts bearing on question whether act was accidental or intentional.	13. Facts bearing on question whether act was accidental or intentional.
16. Existence of course of business when relevant.	14. Existence of course of business when relevant.
ADMISSIONS	**ADMISSIONS**
17. Admission defined.	15. Admission defined.
18. Admission - by party to proceeding or his agent; by suitor in representative character; by party interested in subject-matter; by person from whom interest derived.	16. Admission by party to proceeding or his agent.
19. Admissions by persons whose position must be proved as against party to suit.	17. Admissions by persons whose position must be proved as against party to suit.
20. Admissions by persons expressly referred to by party to suit.	18. Admissions by persons expressly referred to by party to suit.
21. Proof of admissions against persons making them, and by or on their behalf.	19. Proof of admissions against persons making them, and by or on their behalf.
22. When oral admissions as to contents of documents are relevant.	20. When oral admissions as to contents of documents are relevant.

INDIAN EVIDENCE ACT, 1872	BHARATIYA SAKSHYA ADHINIYAM, 2023
22A. When oral admission as to contents of electronic records are relevant.	**DELETED**
23. Admissions in civil cases when relevant.	21. Admissions in civil cases when relevant.
24. Confession caused by inducement, threat or promise, when irrelevant in criminal proceeding.	**22. Confession caused by inducement, threat, coercion or promise, when irrelevant in criminal proceeding. (Change)**
25. Confession to police-officer not to be proved.	23. Confession to police officer. 23(1)
26. Confession by accused while in custody of Police not to be proved against him.	23(2)
27. How much of information received from accused may be proved.	23. Proviso
28. Confession made after removal of impression caused by inducement, threat or promise, relevant.	22. Proviso 1
29. Confession otherwise relevant not to become irrelevant because of promise of secrecy, etc.	22. Proviso 2
30. Consideration of proved confession affecting person making it and others jointly under trial for same offence.	**24. Consideration of proved confession affecting person making it and others jointly under trial for same offence. (Change)**
31. Admissions not conclusive proof, but may estop.	25. Admissions not conclusive proof, but may estop.
STATEMENTS BY PERSONS WHO CANNOT BE CALLED AS WITNESSES	**STATEMENTS BY PERSONS WHO CANNOT BE CALLED AS WITNESSES**

INDIAN EVIDENCE ACT, 1872	BHARATIYA SAKSHYA ADHINIYAM, 2023
32. Cases in which statement of relevant fact by person who is dead or cannot be found, etc., is relevant.	26. **Cases in which statement of relevant fact by person who is dead or cannot be found, etc., is relevant. (Change)**
33. Relevancy of certain evidence for proving, in subsequent proceeding, the truth of facts therein stated.	27. Relevancy of certain evidence for proving, in subsequent proceeding, truth of facts therein stated.
STATEMENTS MADE UNDER SPECIAL CIRCUMSTANCES	**STATEMENTS MADE UNDER SPECIAL CIRCUMSTANCES**
34. Entries in books of account, including when relevant.	28. Entries in books of account when relevant.
35. Relevancy of entry in public record made in performance of duty.	29. Relevancy of entry in public record or an electronic record made in performance of duty.
36. Relevancy of statements in maps, charts and plans.	30. Relevancy of statements in maps, charts and plans.
37. Relevancy of statement as to fact of public nature contained in certain Acts or notifications.	31. **Relevancy of statement as to fact of public nature contained in certain Acts or notifications. (Change)**
38. Relevancy of statements as to any law contained in law-books.	32. **Relevancy of statements as to any law contained in law books including electronic or digital form. (Change)**
HOW MUCH OF A STATEMENT IS TO BE PROVED	**HOW MUCH OF A STATEMENT IS TO BE PROVED**
39. What evidence to be given when statement from part of a conversation, document, electronic record, book or series of letters or papers.	33. What evidence to be given when statement forms part of a conversation, document, electronic record, book or series of letters or papers.

INDIAN EVIDENCE ACT, 1872	BHARATIYA SAKSHYA ADHINIYAM, 2023
JUDGMENTS OF COURTS OF JUSTICE WHEN RELEVANT	**JUDGMENTS OF COURTS WHEN RELEVANT**
40. Previous judgments relevant to bar a second suit or trial.	34. Previous judgments relevant to bar a second suit or trial.
41. Relevancy of certain judgments in probate, etc., jurisdiction.	35. **Relevancy of certain judgments in probate, etc., jurisdiction. (Change)**
42. Relevancy and effect of judgments, orders or decrees, other than those mentioned in section 41.	36. Relevancy and effect of judgments, orders or decrees, other than those mentioned in section 35.
43. Judgments, etc., other than those mentioned in sections 40, 41 and 42, when relevant.	37. Judgments, etc., other than those mentioned in sections 34, 35 and 36 when relevant.
44. Fraud or collusion in obtaining judgment, or incompetency of Court, may be proved.	38. Fraud or collusion in obtaining judgment, or incompetency of Court, may be proved.
OPINIONS OF THIRD PERSONS WHEN RELEVANT	**OPINIONS OF THIRD PERSONS WHEN RELEVANT**
45. Opinions of experts.	39. **Opinions of experts. (Change)** 39(1)
45A. Opinion of Examiner of Electronic Evidence.	39(2)
46. Facts hearing upon opinions of experts.	40. Facts bearing upon opinions of experts.
47. Opinion as to handwriting, when relevant.	41. Opinion as to handwriting and signature, when relevant. 41(1)
47A. Opinion as to digital signature, when relevant.	41(2)
48. Opinion as to existence of right or custom, when relevant.	42. Opinion as to existence of general custom or right, when relevant.

INDIAN EVIDENCE ACT, 1872	BHARATIYA SAKSHYA ADHINIYAM, 2023
49. Opinion as to usages, tenets, etc., when relevant.	43. Opinion as to usages, tenets, etc., when relevant.
50. Opinion on relationship, when relevant.	44. Opinion on relationship, when relevant.
51. Grounds of opinion, when relevant.	45. Grounds of opinion, when relevant.
CHARACTER WHEN RELEVANT	**CHARACTER WHEN RELEVANT**
52. In civil cases character to prove conduct imputed, irrelevant.	46. In civil cases character to prove conduct imputed, irrelevant.
53. In criminal cases previous good character relevant.	47. In criminal cases previous good character relevant.
53A. Evidence of character or previous sexual experience not relevant in certain cases.	48. Evidence of character or previous sexual experience not relevant in certain cases.
54. Previous bad character not relevant, except in reply.	49. Previous bad character not relevant, except in reply.
55. Character as affecting damages.	50. Character as affecting damages.
PART II **ON PROOF** **CHAPTER III** **FACTS WHICH NEED NOT BE PROVED**	**PART III** **ON PROOF** **CHAPTER III** **FACTS WHICH NEED NOT BE PROVED**
56. Fact judicially noticeable need not be proved.	51. Fact judicially noticeable need not be proved.
57. Facts of which Court must take judicial notice.	52. **Facts of which Court shall take judicial notice. (Change)**
58. Facts admitted need not be proved.	53. Facts admitted need not be proved.
CHAPTER IV **OF ORAL EVIDENCE**	**CHAPTER IV** **OF ORAL EVIDENCE**
59. Proof of facts by oral evidence.	54. **Proof of facts by oral evidence. (Change)**

INDIAN EVIDENCE ACT, 1872	BHARATIYA SAKSHYA ADHINIYAM, 2023
60. Oral evidence must be direct.	55. Oral evidence to be direct.
CHAPTER V **OF DOCUMENTARY EVIDENCE**	**CHAPTER V** **OF DOCUMENTARY EVIDENCE**
61. Proof of contents of documents.	56. Proof of contents of documents.
62. Primary evidence.	57. **Primary evidence. (Change)**
63. Secondary evidence.	58. **Secondary evidence. (Change)**
64. Proof of documents by primary evidence.	59. Proof of documents by primary evidence.
65. Cases in which secondary evidence relating to documents may be given.	60. Cases in which secondary evidence relating to documents may be given.
New Section	61. **Electronic or digital record.**
65A. Special provisions as to evidence relating to electronic record.	62. Special provisions as to evidence relating to electronic record.
65B. Admissibility of electronic records.	63. **Admissibility of electronic records. (Change)**
65B (3) (a) by a combination of computers operating over that period; or	**Deleted**
65B (3) (b) by different computers operating in succession over that period; or	**Deleted**
65B (3) (c) by different combinations of computers operating in succession over that period; or	**Deleted**
Deleted	**65B (3) (d) in any other manner involving the successive operation over that period, in whatever order, of one or more computers and one or more combinations of computers.**

INDIAN EVIDENCE ACT, 1872	BHARATIYA SAKSHYA ADHINIYAM, 2023
65B 5 (b) whether in the course of activities carried on by any official, information is supplied with a view to its being stored or processed for the purposes of those activities by a computer operated otherwise than in the course of those activities, that information, if duly supplied to that computer, shall be taken to be supplied to it in the course of those activities;	**Deleted**
66. Rules as to notice to produce.	64. **Rules as to notice to produce. (Change)**
67. Proof of signature and handwriting of person alleged to have signed or written document produced.	65. Proof of signature and handwriting of person alleged to have signed or written document produced.
67A. Proof as to electronic signature.	66. Proof as to electronic signature.
68. Proof of execution of document required by law to be attested.	67. Proof of execution of document required by law to be attested.
69. Proof where no attesting witness found.	68. Proof where no attesting witness found.
70. Admission of execution by party to attested document.	69. Admission of execution by party to attested document.
71. Proof when attesting witness denies the execution.	70. Proof when attesting witness denies execution.
72. Proof of document not required by law to be attested.	71. Proof of document not required by law to be attested.
73. Comparison of signature, writing or seal with others admitted or proved.	72. Comparison of signature, writing or seal with others admitted or proved.
73A. Proof as to verification of digital signature.	73. Proof as to verification of digital signature.

INDIAN EVIDENCE ACT, 1872	BHARATIYA SAKSHYA ADHINIYAM, 2023
PUBLIC DOCUMENTS	**PUBLIC DOCUMENTS**
74. Public documents.	74. **Public and private documents. (Change)** 74(1).
75. Private documents.	74(2).
76. Certified copies of public documents.	75. Certified copies of public documents.
77. Proof of documents by production of certified copies.	76. Proof of documents by production of certified copies.
78. Proof of other official documents.	77. **Proof of other official documents. (Change)**
PRESUMPTIONS AS TO DOCUMENTS	**PRESUMPTIONS AS TO DOCUMENTS**
79. Presumption as to genuineness of certified copies.	78. Presumption as to genuineness of certified copies
80. Presumption as to documents produced as record of evidence.	79. Presumption as to documents produced as record of evidence, etc.
81. Presumption as to Gazettes, newspapers, private Acts of Parliament and other documents. Explanation of S. 90	80. Presumption as to Gazettes, newspapers, and other documents. Explanation
81A. Presumption as to Gazettes in electronic forms. Explanation of S. 90A	81. **Presumption as to Gazettes in electronic or digital record. (Change)** Explanation
82. Presumption as to document admissible in England without proof of seal or signature.	**DELETED**
83. Presumption as to maps or plans made by authority of Government.	82. Presumption as to maps or plans made by authority of Government.
84. Presumption as to collections of laws and reports of decisions.	83. Presumption as to collections of laws and reports of decisions.

INDIAN EVIDENCE ACT, 1872	BHARATIYA SAKSHYA ADHINIYAM, 2023
85. Presumptions as to powers-of-attorney.	84. Presumption as to powers-of-attorney.
85A. Presumption as to electronic agreements.	**85. Presumption as to electronic agreements. (Change)**
85B. Presumption as to electronic records and electronic signatures.	86. Presumption as to electronic records and electronic signatures.
85C. Presumption as to electronic signature certificates.	87. Presumption as to Electronic Signature Certificates.
86. Presumption as to certified copies of foreign judicial records.	88. Presumption as to certified copies of foreign judicial records.
87. Presumption as to books, maps and charts.	89. Presumption as to books, maps and charts.
88. Presumption as to telegraphic messages.	**DELETED**
88A. Presumption as to electronic messages.	90. Presumption as to electronic messages.
89. Presumption as to due execution, etc., of documents not produced.	91. Presumption as to due execution, etc., of documents not produced.
90. Presumption as to documents thirty years old.	92. Presumption as to documents thirty years old.
90A. Presumption as to electronic records five years old.	93. Presumption as to electronic records five years old.
CHAPTER VI **OF THE EXCLUSION OF ORAL BY DOCUMENTARY EVIDENCE**	**CHAPTER VI** **OF THE EXCLUSION OF ORAL EVIDENCE BY DOCUMENTARY EVIDENCE**
91. Evidence of terms of contracts, grants and other dispositions of property reduced to form of document.	94. Evidence of terms of contracts, grants and other dispositions of property reduced to form of document.
92. Exclusion of evidence of oral agreement.	95. Exclusion of evidence of oral agreement.

INDIAN EVIDENCE ACT, 1872	BHARATIYA SAKSHYA ADHINIYAM, 2023
93. Exclusion of evidence to explain or amend ambiguous document.	96. Exclusion of evidence to explain or amend ambiguous document.
94. Exclusion of evidence against application of document to existing facts.	97. Exclusion of evidence against application of document to existing facts.
95. Evidence as to document unmeaning in reference to existing facts.	98. Evidence as to document unmeaning in reference to existing facts.
96. Evidence as to application of language which can apply to one only of several persons.	99. Evidence as to application of language which can apply to one only of several persons.
97. Evidence as to application of language to one of two sets of facts, to neither of which the whole correctly applies.	100. Evidence as to application of language to one of two sets of facts, to neither of which the whole correctly applies.
98. Evidence as to meaning of illegible characters, etc.	101. **Evidence as to meaning of illegible characters, etc. (Change)**
99. Who may give evidence of agreement varying terms of document.	102. Who may give evidence of agreement varying terms of document.
100. Saving of provisions of Indian Succession Act relating to wills.	103. Saving of provisions of Indian Succession Act relating to wills.
PART III **PRODUCTION AND EFFECT OF EVIDENCE** **CHAPTER VII** **OF THE BURDEN OF PROOF**	**PART IV** **PRODUCTION AND EFFECT OF EVIDENCE** **CHAPTER VII** **OF THE BURDEN OF PROOF**
101. Burden of proof.	104. Burden of proof.
102. On whom burden of proof lies.	105. On whom burden of proof lies.
103. Burden of proof as to particular fact.	106. Burden of proof as to particular fact.
104. Burden of proving fact to be proved to make evidence admissible.	107. Burden of proving fact to be proved to make evidence admissible.

INDIAN EVIDENCE ACT, 1872	BHARATIYA SAKSHYA ADHINIYAM, 2023
105. Burden of proving that case of accused comes within exceptions.	108. Burden of proving that case of accused comes within exceptions.
106. Burden of proving fact especially within knowledge.	109. Burden of proving fact especially within knowledge.
107. Burden of proving death of person known to have been alive within thirty years.	110. Burden of proving death of person known to have been alive within thirty years.
108. Burden of proving that person is alive who has not been heard of for seven years.	111. Burden of proving that person is alive who has not been heard of for seven years.
109. Burden of proof as to relationship in the cases of partners, landlord and tenant, principal and agent.	112. Burden of proof as to relationship in the cases of partners, landlord and tenant, principal and agent.
110. Burden of proof as to ownership.	113. Burden of proof as to ownership.
111. Proof of good faith in transactions where one party is in relation of active confidence.	114. Proof of good faith in transactions where one party is in relation of active confidence.
111A. Presumption as to certain offences.	115. Presumption as to certain offences.
112. Birth during marriage, conclusive proof of legitimacy.	116. Birth during marriage, conclusive proof of legitimacy.
113. Proof of cession of territory.	**DELETED**
113A. Presumption as to abetment of suicide by a married woman.	117. Presumption as to abetment of suicide by a married woman.
113B. Presumption as to dowry death.	118. Presumption as to dowry death.
114. Court may presume existence of certain facts.	119. Court may presume existence of certain facts.
114A. Presumption as to absence of consent in certain prosecution for rape	120. **Presumption as to absence of consent in certain prosecution for rape. (Change)**

INDIAN EVIDENCE ACT, 1872	BHARATIYA SAKSHYA ADHINIYAM, 2023
CHAPTER VIII **ESTOPPEL**	**CHAPTER VIII** **ESTOPPEL**
115. Estoppel.	121. Estoppel.
116. Estoppel of tenants and of licensee of person in possession.	122. Estoppel of tenants and of licensee of person in possession.
117. Estoppel of acceptor of bill of exchange, bailee or licensee.	123. Estoppel of acceptor of bill of exchange, bailee or licensee.
CHAPTER IX **OF WITNESSES**	**CHAPTER IX** **OF WITNESSES**
118. Who may testify.	124. Who may testify.
119. Witness unable to communicate verbally.	125. Witness unable to communicate verbally.
120. Parties to civil suit, and their wives or husbands. Husband or wife of person under criminal trial.	126. Competency of husband and wife as witnesses in certain cases.
121. Judges and Magistrates.	127. Judges and Magistrates.
122. Communications during marriage.	128. Communications during marriage.
123. Evidence as to affairs of State.	129. Evidence as to affairs of State.
124. Official communications.	130. Official communications.
125. Information as to commission of offences.	131. Information as to commission of offences.
126. Professional communications.	132. Professional Communications. 132(1) (2)
127. Section 126 to apply to interpreters, etc.	132(3)
128. Privilege not waived by volunteering evidence.	133. Privilege not waived by volunteering evidence.
129. Confidential communications with legal advisers.	134. Confidential communication with legal advisers.
130. Production of title-deeds of witness not a party.	135. Production of title-deeds of witness not a party.

INDIAN EVIDENCE ACT, 1872	BHARATIYA SAKSHYA ADHINIYAM, 2023
131. Production of documents or electronic records which another person, having possession, could refuse to produce.	136. Production of documents or electronic records which another person, having possession, could refuse to produce.
132. Witness not excused from answering on ground that answer will criminate.	137. Witness not excused from answering on ground that answer will criminate.
133. Accomplice.	138. **Accomplice. (Change)**
134. Number of witnesses.	139. Number of witnesses.
CHAPTER X **OF THE EXAMINATION OF WITNESSES**	**CHAPTER X** **OF EXAMINATION OF WITNESSES**
135. Order of production and examination of witnesses.	140. Order of production and examination of witnesses.
136. Judge to decide as to admissibility of evidence.	141. Judge to decide as to admissibility of evidence.
137. Examination-in-chief.	142. Examination of witnesses.
138. Order of examinations.	143. Order of examinations.
139. Cross-examination of person called to produce a document.	144. Cross-examination of person called to produce a document.
140. Witnesses to character.	145. Witnesses to character.
141. Leading questions.	146. Leading questions. 146(1).
142. When they must not be asked.	146(2), 146(3).
143. When they may be asked.	146(4).
144. Evidence as to matters in writing.	147. Evidence as to matters in writing.
145. Cross-examination as to previous statements in writing.	148. Cross-examination as to previous statements in writing.
146. Questions lawful in cross-examination.	149. Questions lawful in cross-examination.
147. When witness to be compelled to answer.	150. When witness to be compelled to answer.

INDIAN EVIDENCE ACT, 1872	BHARATIYA SAKSHYA ADHINIYAM, 2023
148. Court to decide when question shall be asked and when witness compelled to answer.	151. Court to decide when question shall be asked and when witness compelled to answer.
149. Question not to be asked without reasonable grounds.	152. Question not to be asked without reasonable grounds.
150. Procedure of Court in case of question being asked without reasonable grounds.	153. Procedure of Court in case of question being asked without reasonable grounds.
151. Indecent and scandalous questions.	154. Indecent and scandalous questions.
152. Questions intended to insult or annoy.	155. Questions intended to insult or annoy.
153. Exclusion of evidence to contradict answers to questions testing veracity.	156. Exclusion of evidence to contradict answers to questions testing veracity.
154. Question by party to his own witness.	157. Question by party to his own witness.
155. Impeaching credit of witness.	158. Impeaching credit of witness.
156. Questions tending to corroborate evidence of relevant fact, admissible.	159. Questions tending to corroborate evidence of relevant fact, admissible.
157. Former statements of witness may be proved to corroborate later testimony as to same fact.	160. Former statements of witness may be proved to corroborate later testimony as to same fact.
158. What matters may be proved in connection with proved statement relevant under section 32 or 33.	161. What matters may be proved in connection with proved statement relevant under section 26 or 27.
159. Refreshing memory.	162. Refreshing memory.
160. Testimony to facts stated in document mentioned in section 159.	163. Testimony to facts stated in document mentioned in section 162
161. Right of adverse party as to writing used to refresh memory.	164. Right of adverse party as to writing used to refresh memory.

INDIAN EVIDENCE ACT, 1872	BHARATIYA SAKSHYA ADHINIYAM, 2023
162. Production of documents.	165. **Production of documents. (Change)**
163. Giving, as evidence, of document called for and produced on notice.	166. Giving, as evidence, of document called for and produced on notice.
164. Using, as evidence, of document production of which was refused on notice.	167. Using, as evidence, of document production of which was refused on notice.
165. Judge's power to put questions or order production.	168. **Judge's power to put questions or order production. (Change)**
166. Power of jury or assessors to put questions.	**DELETED**
CHAPTER XI **OF IMPROPER ADMISSION AND REJECTION OF EVIDENCE**	**CHAPTER XI** **OF IMPROPER ADMISSION AND REJECTION OF EVIDENCE**
167. No new trial for improper admission or rejection of evidence.	169. No new trial for improper admission or rejection of evidence.
	CHAPTER XII **REPEAL AND SAVINGS**
New Section	170. Repeal and savings.

Note: For reference only.

www.ingramcontent.com/pod-product-compliance
Lightning Source LLC
Chambersburg PA
CBHW031408250726
48656CB00002B/531